Women Who Wear Only Themselves

Women Who Wear Only Themselves

Four Travelers on Their Sacred Journeys

Arundhathi Subramaniam

HarperOne
An Imprint of HarperCollins*Publishers*

Originally published in India in 2021 by Speaking Tiger

First HarperOne edition published in 2025

Designed by Janet Evans-Scanlon

Library of Congress Cataloging-in-Publication Data has been applied for.

ISBN 978-0-06-338589-4

24 25 26 27 28 LBC 5 4 3 2 1

People,
male and female,
blush when a cloth covering their shame
comes loose.
     When the lord of lives
lives drowned without a face
in the world, how can you be modest?

When all the world is the eye of the lord,
onlooking everywhere, what can you
cover and conceal?

—Akka Mahadevi
   (translated by A. K. Ramanujan)

CONTENTS

Home

Give me a home
that isn't mine,
where I can slip in and out of rooms
without a trace,
never worrying
about the plumbing,
the color of the curtains,
the cacophony of books by the bedside.

A home that I can wear lightly,
where the rooms aren't clogged
with yesterday's conversations,
where the self doesn't bloat
to fill in the crevices.

A home, like this body,
so alien when I try to belong,
so hospitable
when I decide I'm just visiting.

AUTHOR'S NOTE

Sometimes when I look out of the eighteenth-floor window of this Manhattan apartment, I wonder in some amazement at how I landed up here.

"Landed up" is not quite the mot juste, I'm aware. I'm a seasoned enough traveler to know that. It's just that life has a way of changing the scenery in ways that never cease to startle.

Strangely, one of my earliest life memories is also of a window. Through its spacious geometry, patterned by an ornate cursive grill, I looked out at a vast peepul tree and a distant smudge of ocean. I wondered then, too, at how I landed up there. That was accompanied by a sadness that I could not name. It is a sadness three-year-olds know well.

When I wrote the poem "Home" (that opens this book), the year was 2003. I had no idea how prescient the poem would prove to be. But poems, I've found, are invariably smarter than I am.

I believed at the time that my life was reasonably settled.

Or, at least, somewhat settled in its unsettlement. I lived in a high-octane harbor city of many names: Bombay/Mumbai/Bambai. I had work, an address, a partner, three cats. I spent my life wandering the beguiling hysteria of the city streets, inhaling its smoggy air, meeting friends over coffees and poetry readings, where we gnashed our teeth over cultural politics, gender injustice, bad art, our great messy subcontinent of demons. None of us was particularly at ease in our own skins, but we called that being edgy. Perhaps we even derived an identity from all that unease.

And yet, a niggling sense of being an impostor in a bodysuit never quite went away. Some days, I felt like I was in costume. Other days, in armor—clunky, but necessary. I knew, too, that even chain mail, helmet, and saber wouldn't prepare me for the crazy, seething big city I lived in.

The bodysuit had its moments. Role-play, I found, could even be exhilarating. But behind it was a hunger. A mounting, nameless hunger for something more. Something deeper, truer, less heavy, less changeable. My home. My tribe. My garment. Myself.

Nothing original about any of that, of course. But I didn't know that at the time.

And so, my closet life began. By day, I was a poet, writer, journalist, curator. In the dark womb of the closet, I was a desperate, undignified seeker. Poetry offered insight. Reading philosophy offered consolation. My love of theater and dance offered beauty. But all those churning questions about truth, loss, perishability, and unbelonging were gathering momentum. And an unexplained near-death experience—a kind of crash course in emptiness—in 1997 gave those questions greater urgency.

I turned to reading the mystics—the only ones who spoke of this indefinable hunger in a way that resonated. It was an odd condition. I was surrounded by people with whom it was perfectly acceptable to discuss Dostoevsky and Simone de Beauvoir, and rage against the heavy-handedness of the Indian state. But to talk of the spirit? Apostasy.

I could see why. After all, who in modern metropolitan India of the 1980s and '90s wanted to rehash those tedious clichés about the exotic East? Who wanted to join the Big Brothers of the planet who had reduced the mystery of faith to dogma, hierarchy, exclusivity? Who wanted to be seen gravitating toward the embarrassingly trite self-help literature that was beginning to flood the bookstores? Who, for god's sake, wanted to be seen as *religious*? As for the divine, what was that anyway? The gods invented by organized religion seemed to be a chronically territorial bunch, oozing testosterone, jostling for supremacy. Not terribly inspiring.

And still, the mystics seemed to be on to something. I heard it in the hoarseness of their voices, their refusal to join the dots, their dazed inarticulacy.

And then, in 2004, I met my spiritual guide.

It felt (as I wrote in a poem) like I "opened my coffee percolator" and found my roof flying off. After seven years of seeking, I exhaled. This was someone who understood, without my having to say a word. There was magic in the air. If life had been stodgy prose, it was now lyric poetry.

In 2010, I left a job, a city, a relationship (that had crumbled a while ago), and multiple professional identities that had mattered to me, and moved to an ashram. It wasn't heroic. And it wasn't self-destructive, as some of my friends probably believed. It just felt necessary. I was following the call of the wild. Or the call of home. I wasn't sure which. Perhaps they were the same thing.

And yet, home didn't mean a simple change of address either. The ashram was a place of rapid self-reclamation. But it emphatically wasn't a cozy nest, a sanctuary in which you settled into snoozy couch-potatohood; it was more a laboratory in which you were compelled to be both scientist and experiment. What it offered me was a place to breathe and recharge as the fragments of my life swirled around me, wild, turbulent, sometimes ecstatic. My pillow was wet with tears some nights, but it also felt oddly right to be lost.

This was a new kind of "lost." Earlier, being lost was a kind of pain. There was desperation in that absence of anchor. So, when I discovered a spiritual path of my own, it felt like I had finally been "found." I could see why so many sacred poems spoke of quest as a game of hide-and-seek. Now I was lost again, but this was a darkly euphoric freefall, almost as if I had authored the architecture of my own unmaking. And through it all, I felt the sure-footedness of my guru's presence and guidance.

In that state without reference points, I also found my tribe. No, it wasn't the fellow yoga practitioner. And no, it wasn't the skeptic. It wasn't the devotee. And it wasn't the agnostic. I couldn't handle the sanctimony of the believer any more than I could handle the arrogance of the rationalist. I belonged, I realized, to the tribe of the bewildered. Those who choose wonder over borrowed conviction. Those whose beliefs have often been stunned into silence. And sometimes, into song.

Poetry began to return.

The travel never abated. I wandered from ashram room to literature conferences around the world, from friends' homes in different cities to my parents' welcoming abode. I didn't fully belong anywhere. At the same time, I found flickering moments of kinship in the gazes of people. Many shared their life stories with an unguardedness that amazed me. I grew grateful for these campfires in unexpected places.

Would I ever find my home, I once asked my guru. His response was brief: "Learn to enjoy the life of a vagabond."

I began to see what that meant.

Vagabondage became a spiritual path. It wasn't about notching up frequent-flyer miles, or writing glamorous transit-lounge travelogues. It was about learning to live as a guest, not an entitled host. I learned to be grateful to those who welcomed me to a meal, offered me their guest rooms, sometimes trusted me with their house keys. I looked wistfully into their brightly lit homes at times, my nose pressed, figuratively, against their window panes, aware that I was an outsider to their settled lives. But sometimes, I found them looking at me wistfully too. For somewhere, people seem to instinctively recognize the freedom of mendicancy, even in its unlikely modern-day manifestations. It is probably why Indian householders traditionally offered wandering *parivrajakas* (sacred travelers) food and shelter. They knew they were both part of the same ecosystem, each, in their own way, sustained by the other.

A poem by the Italian poet Salvatore Quasimodo has haunted me for decades:

Everyone stands alone at the heart of the world
pierced by a ray of sunlight
and suddenly it's evening.

The business of living can be opaque, terrifyingly solitary. Yet, there is a ray of sunlight on which each of us is impaled. That is our spine, our own very singular way of belonging to time and transcendence. Evening comes sooner than we think. But when it does, I would like to know I have tried to live a chosen life, not a borrowed one. I hope to have been my own quiet axis between earth and sky. My own conscious bridge between flesh and spirit. My own hyphen between diverse experiences. I hope to have been my own person—fallible, but whole.

Author's Note

I began coming home to myself.

I found that I didn't have to buy into the tired dualities of the outside world. I didn't have to choose between external definitions of spirituality and worldliness. Between cultural rootedness and world citizenship. Between mind and heart. Between secular and sacred. Between traditional and contemporary. Between this and that. Either and or.

I could be both. Because I *am* both. And consciously being both, I realize, is the glory of being human.

The external plot of my life shifted. It continues to. My poems changed. They grew more bullet-holed by silences. My prose began to explore sacred journeys, my own understanding of the radical inner core of *bhakti*, or devotion. I wrote now more from experience, less, it seemed, from opinion and hardened attitude. Mind and heart seemed more in conversation than before.

In time, love happened. Marriage brought me to America in 2018. New York became yet another home. At the same time, a deep cultural affinity and a calling I cannot name impels me to return to India. Since I work with words, I spend much of my time reading, writing, and traveling. But since I work with silences too, my solitary time remains a fiercely guarded priority.

It has been a journey from unbelonging to voluntary exile, from dispossession to gratitude for many homes, a state of multiple citizenship.

And it's not over yet.

Author's Note

Along the way, my ideas of home have changed. Once I learned to be a traveler and guest, I learned that I could become a host too. Not a lordly host. Just one who knows there are many rightful owners to the same kingdom. "Between cringing vassal state / and walled medieval town" there is a way to inhabit the self. I'm beginning to see that.

My notion of my tribe has changed too. I have always seen family more as invented than inherited. I have considered close friends to be my clan. But once I learned that I belonged to the tribe of the "born-again bewildered"—the joyfully uncertain, the wonderers rather than the white-knuckled sentinels of opinion—I began finding relatives everywhere. Frequently in the most unforeseen places.

I've also picked up some old hitchhiking secrets along the way. When you're dazed by the vertiginous business of picking yourself up and moving on, there is only one place where you can find your home: yourself. And when you don't really belong anywhere, there is only one place you can possibly claim as your own: the world.

I forget often. But remembering is a kind of homecoming.

And that helps.

The strange thing about love

is that it melts you

into an amateur,

never again a professional
      even
         on the subject of yourself.

*

The strange thing about love

is that you disagree,

disagree wildly,

and then figure it's wiser

to dance.

*

The strange thing about love

is that it evicts you
from the land of echoes
you thought was home

and leads you to
friends

sitting
under the stars

in ancient
bewilderment.

When God is a Traveller

(wondering about Kartikeya, Muruga, Subramania, my
namesake)

Trust the god
back from his travels,

his voice wholegrain
        (and chamomile),
his wisdom neem,
        his peacock, sweaty-plumed,
        drowsing in the shadows.

Trust him
who sits wordless on park benches
listening to the cries of children
fading into the dusk,
        his gaze emptied of vagrancy,
        his heart of ownership.

Trust him
who has seen enough—
revolutions, promises, the desperate light
of shopping malls, hospital rooms,
manifestos, theologies, the iron taste
of blood, the great craters in the middle
        of love.

Trust him
who no longer begrudges
his brother his prize,
his parents their partisanship.

Trust him
whose race is run,
whose journey remains,

who stands fluid-stemmed
knowing he is the tree
that bears fruit, festive
             with sun.

Trust him
who recognizes you—
auspicious, abundant, battle-scarred,
                alive—
and knows from where you come.

Trust the god
ready to circle the world all over again
this time for no reason at all

other than to see it
through your eyes.

Preface

The primary motivation behind this book is simple. Thirst. Hopefully, a shared thirst.

As a seeker, I have spent years thirsting for conversations. With spiritual teachers, with fellow travelers committed to the life of the spirit. I cannot complain. My life has been rich in conversations.

I have had conversations with seekers of various persuasions. I have spent long hours listening to the yogi and mystic who later became my guru. I have eavesdropped on countless conversations with mystics in books—Shirdi Sai Baba, J. Krishnamurti, Ramana Maharishi, Nisargadatta Maharaj, Osho. I've even imagined the lapping waters of the Hooghly quieting to listen to the extraordinary exchanges between Ramakrishna Paramahamsa and his disciples.

But another kind of thirst remained.

A thirst for conversations with *women*. Women of our

times. Contemporary women. Women who improvise their way through their lives even as we speak. Women walking the spiritual path right now—sometimes confidently, sometimes haltingly, but who still feel compelled to walk it.

The Indian spiritual landscape is not devoid of women. We are routinely reminded of an illustrious litany: Maitreyi, Gargi, Andal, Karaikal Ammaiyar, Akka Mahadevi, Janabai, Muktabai, Bahinabai, Lal Ded, Rupa Bhavani, Gangasati, Meerabai. The list is long and varied. There are well-known figures in more recent times too, from the twentieth-century mystics, Anandamayi Ma and The Mother of Pondicherry, to contemporary guru Mata Amritanandamayi. Remarkable women. Beacons for many even today.

But what of the *quiet* women? Women who never founded large institutions, women who never created legions of devotees or social media acolytes to document their lives in hagiography and legend, and sing their praises in folk song and sacred verse? What of them?

There was no crusading zeal that motivated this book. There was no schematic design. No spirit of advocacy. But there was a longing to listen to the voices of lesser-known women—women who choose to live in relative seclusion and shadow, and yet burn brightly. Women whom I met, accidentally, in the course of my own journey, and who generously allowed me a glimpse of their light. Something shifted within me after each of these chance encounters. I did not leave any of them unmoved.

Preface

These women made no effort to impress. They were gracious enough to share their life journeys, without trying to flaunt their attainments, win recruits, or garner publicity. I am a seasoned listener and instantly alert to subtle attempts to broker deals. There were no bargains being hatched here. I write about these conversations primarily because they were so remarkably free of agenda.

These women are not spiritual celebrities. Some of them have their own local following, but they are not in the glare of the spotlight. Their abodes are not mandatory halts in Lonely Planet guides for international pilgrims.

Their self-containment intrigued me. They will never rank among the metaphysicians and sectarian founders (all male—and dutifully archived in treatises on the exoteric history of religious traditions). Instead, they are among those who leave behind a fragrance that is seldom acknowledged, indeed seldom noticed. They remind me of the many women who have walked the world down the centuries, undocumented—sometimes perhaps content to be so. And yet, I cannot help feeling a twinge when I think of them—those consigned to the junk folders of history by steamrolling narratives. That twinge was also one of the reasons behind this book.

My initial encounters with the women in this book were unplanned. I happened to have spent large swaths of time in southern India in the past decade, and so, not surprisingly, that is where these meetings happened. They are not meant to represent the religious plurality of the Indian subcontinent, although I do believe that they reveal the still-unvanquished hospitality of vision that characterizes its spiritual ethos. Each conversation was as different as the woman in question, accounting for the very different stylistic texture and tone of each essay in this book.

These women inspired me. Sometimes by what they said. Sometimes by how they said it. Sometimes by their words, sometimes by their presence. Always by their independence. Each of them reminded me—in their own, very particular ways—of that old and beautiful metaphor of the lotus in the marsh.

The terror of uncertainty is more blazingly evident in our world than it ever has been. To carve a path between the certitudes of a frozen faith and the dogmas of arid materialism can be challenging. I marveled at how these women held their own in a world so conceptually fragmented. A world that divides the material and the spiritual into such impermeable categories. How did these women tune in to their own inner guidance? How did they come to terms with that simple but oddly elusive truth: that we are both flesh *and* spirit? That we do not have to masquerade as simply one or the other?

Above all, how did they find their freedom in a world where a spiritual ecosystem is particularly hard to find? What *is* a spiritual ecosystem, someone once asked me. One where spiritual seekers aren't apologetic about who they are, I told her. Where they are encouraged to explore, to question fearlessly. Where they are not bullied by purveyors of faith into conclusion. Or by votaries of reason into a knee-jerk scorn for anything beyond the ken of their rational minds. One in which the inner journey is not seen as escapist but as enriching—both for the seeker and the world she inhabits.

For a long while, I have wanted to be among those who live close to the blazing fire that animates a faith.

Not the sentries and spokespersons, but the seekers, the sadhakas. Those whose lives have little to do with the appurtenances of religious identity.

I feel a need to speak of them, because they are the spiritual axis of a living tradition. They do not have recourse to public relations agents and marketing managers; indeed, they are unlikely to seek them. They often opt for the murmur over the megaphone. They choose to drop their voices, rather than try to outshout the racket. They manage—through the din of social media, through the rant of political rhetoric of every hue—to be themselves. They are the unsung reasons why a faith endures.

A faith would be a heap of bones without this anima, this volcanic inner core. And yet, the defenders of sectarian ghettoes and identity politics speak so little of that heart center—the center without which there would be no faith to speak of.

The mystical experience has been viewed in such diverse ways that to define it is to falsify it. Some speak of it as union with an ultimate reality, and others speak of it as self-dissolution. Some speak of rapture, and others of freedom. For some, it is a thunderclap moment of transcendence; for others, a subtle inner alignment with "the way things are," an abiding state of awareness or presence. For some, it is a gentle unfoldment; for others, it is a radical turnaround in consciousness. For some, it is preceded by an incurable homesickness, an unnameable longing for expansion and extinction all at once; for others, it is a crash landing into an ultimate truth, quiet and irrefutable, with no apparent reason. For some, this ultimate truth is utter emptiness; for others, it is plenitude. And there are still others who don't see much difference between the two.

The general consensus, however, is that mysticism points to a state of firsthand experience rather than secondhand wisdom, direct knowing rather than academic knowledge. While the popular view sees it as synonymous with out-of-body experiences, states of trance, vision and possession, most insiders would agree that these are accoutrements to the real thing. The real mystical awakening, they tell us, can, at times, be an unfussy business—a deepening realization rather than a single big bang. More remarkable than the "event" is the transformation it leaves in its wake: a marked rise in freedom, joy, equanimity, inclusiveness, an absence of dogmatism. In a few cases, there seems to be the alchemical ability to awaken others to the experience as well. Such people become spiritual guides, teachers, shamans, gurus.

Preface

Despite the strangeness of the word, there are several doorways to the mystical in everyday life. Philosopher Mircea Eliade speaks of the ordeals of suffering, death, and rebirth that happen recurrently during the human life cycle, reminding us that there are multiple daily triggers for profound inner transformation. Even moments of intense joy or beauty, the mystic poets tell us, can sow the seeds of a sudden and irrevocable shift in perspective, an exultant awakening.

The challenge is to be able to walk through the doorway *consciously*. The seasoned mystics seem to be able to live on both sides of the gates, in an effortless state of dual citizenship. But for many others, these doors can seem terrifying. They can be experienced as gaping holes, tears, and discontinuities in the fabric of life, a confrontation with an existence from which all conferred meaning has been evacuated, gouged out.

"People who love the divine go around with holes in their hearts, and inside the hole is the universe," writes scholar Peter Kingsley. "And there is a great secret: we all have that missingness deep inside us. The only difference between us and the mystics is that they learn to face what we are running from."

While remnants of the mystical are to be found in religious traditions across the board, these are often relegated to the fringes. This is not surprising. Individual awakenings are too destabilizing for clergies of most stripes. Exiling the mystical to the margins is ironic, however, given that the mystical insight lies at the *very core* of any religious tradition. The rest is window dressing.

Window displays can be diverting, of course. They offer the comfort of identity, the consolation of belonging, the beauty of ritual, the seductions of scriptural authority. Contemporary spiritual teacher Mooji calls it the "fish market at the gate of heaven"—a seductive place where many set up residence for lifetimes.

And yet, there are a few who seek more. Who seek the moltenness of the ur-experience, the wild aliveness that burns in the hidden sanctum of every tradition. The sap that vitalizes the very tree of life.

My fascination is with those who face the missingness. These who choose to live close to the naked-wire questions of living and dying. These who are branded, sometimes charred, by these questions, and yet never step away. Externally, they may live on the margins; internally, they stand close to the kernel. Indeed, the margins are often where the kernel is. For many individuals down history have awakened without paying the subscription fee to any faith.

I first grew interested in women mystics in 2003 during a hermetic writers' residency in Scotland where I found myself reading about the Christian mystics—Angela of Foligno, Hildegard of Bingen, Julian of Norwich, Teresa of Avila, Catherine of Siena, Simone Weil. Later, when I rediscovered the legacy of the bhakti poets, I found myself tuning in to the female voices with deepening curiosity. Women seekers began to emerge more vividly in my poems as I followed the mythic trails of the Sanskrit classical heroine Shakuntala and the Tamil crone poet Avvaiyar in their journeys toward wholeness. Mythology is laden with male questor myths, but the female questors are more elusive. They often feature as piecemeal cameos, as the object of the search rather than its subject. I found I had to "dream" my way into their lives—an exercise in reverie and poetry that I found to be a rich and exciting journey.

Of course, this fascination wasn't surprising. I was a woman. I was a seeker. I knew the destination of life's pilgrimage had nothing to do with gender. "The self that hovers between is neither man nor woman," says the tenth-century mystic poet Devara Dasimayya in an iconic poem translated by A. K. Ramanujan. However, the process of getting to that self is different—qualitatively different—for different people. This I did know.

And how could it be otherwise? I remember being particularly struck in my university years by the feminist Christian theologian Valerie Saiving Goldstein's statement that if the male "sin" was hubris, the female counterpart could well be "a dependence on others for one's self-definition." That struck a deep chord. I knew the innumerable ways in which women were routinely encouraged to fritter away personal power. I was familiar with the subtle and not-so-subtle ways in which they continued to be trivialized, damned with faint praise for speaking the "soft" language of the heart, the many contexts in which they were called on to play appeasers and people-pleasers, compelled to broker a cheap peace rather than a more profound harmony. I was only too familiar with the self-doubt and self-esteem issues with which so many of them grappled. I had known them.

I had *been* them.

But I also knew otherwise. I also knew many who had turned pigeonholes into possibilities. I knew those who combined empathy with empowerment, sensitivity with strength. I knew women who embodied a compassion that emphatically wasn't cowardice, who spoke a language of assertion that wasn't conquest, who retained spine but refused to turn rigid—those who knew, in short, how to bend but not break. And as I started distinguishing between dynamic receptivity and meek submission, and as I sought a deeper language of integration—one that wasn't about *talking* wisdom, but *embodying* it—I grew deeply interested in women on the path.

The questions intensified. What languages of self-reclamation resonated with women today? How did they negotiate the routine decrees to subdue the ego, enjoined by every faith? When asked to surrender a self that many had seldom been taught to value, what was the value of that surrender? How did they differentiate between conscious surrender and unconscious servitude? Between a deeply healing resolution and an easy peace? Between patience and passivity? Between being devotee and doormat? And what of the clichés of spirituality that women are expected to rehash more than anyone else—the meekness, the asexuality, the blandness (where the appearance of a boiled egg helps—and perhaps a taste for little else as well)?

Then there were the other questions. How did women refuel these journeys of sometimes terrifying aloneness? What nourished them? What made them live out these parallel lives? What made them hang in there?

And as the questions deepened, so did the conversations. On a spiritual path, one meets a variety of people—the experience junkies, the zealots, the ego-trippers, the self-conscious new initiates. There are also the many wise and wonderful questors who find transformative possibilities in householder lives.

But there are wilder and lonelier trails too.

In his poem "Poet, Lover, Birdwatcher," the poet Nissim Ezekiel speaks of "deserted lanes . . . where the rivers flow / in silence near the source, or by a shore, / remote and thorny like the heart's dark floor." It is here that another kind of sighting happens. It is here that you find those whose lives have been so profoundly altered that they seem to inhabit their very bodies differently.

There is no way to measure their authenticity, so you resort to a more primal olfactory sense. You sniff. You wait. Ezekiel's haunting poem tells us what we might find in these places as remote and intimate as the human heart:

And there the women slowly turn around,
Not only flesh and bone but myths of light

With darkness at the core, and sense is found
By poets lost in crooked, restless flight,
The deaf can hear, the blind recover sight.

And this, I suppose, is what the women of this book offered me—a contraband of radiance that I wanted in some way to smuggle into the printed page.

Individually, these women vary widely from one another. And yet, there are convergences.

Almost all of them speak of spirited relationships with their spiritual guides; of fear and doubt, sometimes social derision; of their quest for a language of their own; of desolation and abandonment; of being rescued by the suddenness of the sacred. All of them speak of the spiritual and the deeply human in the same breath.

They pursue the path of the ineffable with a somewhat terrifying tenacity. They explore the inner life but never confuse it with the jingoism or intolerance that has pervaded so many religious traditions. At the same time, they are not cowed by a worldview that is often indifferent, cynical, or patronizing about matters of faith.

They are not islands. They acknowledge interdependence on many levels. They are indebted to their guides, but their relationship with them is far from sycophantic. And they operate with the kind of inspired ad-hocism that has been the ancient strength of the spiritual culture of this land—accounting for its resilience in the absence of any unitary institution or scripture. They also operate the way women in so many parts of the world often do—intimately, informally, often anonymously. I felt the need to document them not because of their spiritual attainments (which I am not equipped to assess), but because of their crazy devotion to an inner calling.

More fundamentally, I believe there is a need that conversation fulfills in seekers across the board. I have been such a seeker, searching, sometimes desperately, for a language of clues. Some sign of a road having been walked before. Of a road unfolding in a world we can recognize as our own. Some sign that the universe has ears.

It is not just women seekers who need to hear this. Others do too.

Spiritual seekers are, as a rule, thirsty people. Thirsty for stories that suggest that the road less taken is worth taking. That the path less trodden offers its own recompense. I believe the women in this book will offer these reminders to omnivorous seekers everywhere.

For these are exceptional women. Women who do not offer sops or greeting-card homilies, but a hard-earned wisdom, as they navigate their lives of daily reinvention. Women of grit, women of imagination. Women who do not offer conclusion, but continuum—glimpses of life lived out in the present continuous. Women who know faith not by obedience to theory or scriptural scholarship, but through lived experience. Quiet, daily experience. Women who have cast aside costume. Women who refuse to wear borrowed plumes—of passively inherited faith or unexamined piety.

Women who wear—or seek to wear—only themselves.

Finally, a few words about the deepest personal impetus behind this book.

Without consciously acknowledging the Divine Feminine, my life would have been unbalanced, lopsided. I needed the guru principle to remind me that derailment can be a kind of freedom. I needed the goddess to imbue a joyful sensuality into that discovery. The guru was the trapdoor that opened up and plunged me into a dark and ecstatic place of discovery; he is the guide who continues to teach me the crazy art of freefall. The goddess was the one who taught me that the trapdoor under my feet and the gates that open into the outer world aren't so different, after all.

She has been the lubricant, the ally at my elbow, the whisper in my ear, the voice of my heart that told me that the inner world and the outer, mukti and samsara, aren't at war.

I know Devi as a deity who lives in a temple. I also know her as inner experience. If the guru is both person and presence, the goddess is idol and energy all at once. I love the theism of this relationship: the license to relate to her as divine mother and friend. At the same time, she infuses me with an energy that feels like my own, reminding me that we are deeply related under the skin.

As deity, she is explosively engaged. She is unafraid to reach out and swarm into your bloodstream, to engage herself in the minutiae of your life. She loves the particular. She loves the singular. She is universality itself. And yet, she surges between the abstract and concrete with an impunity, with a gorgeous elegance—the kind that, I suppose, only a goddess would be capable of.

The guru is the road map back to yourself. The goddess is a reminder that you'd never left.

Since this book is a mosaic of women's voices, I dedicate it to Devi—and to the many fascinating women to whom she continues to lead me.

Goddess II

after Linga Bhairavi

In her burning rainforest
silence is so alive
you can hear

listening.

Textile

Some days
nothing in your wardrobe satisfies,
not the heat-maddened ikats, not the secular pastels.

There's no season you can call your own.

Like others
you wait
in queues
for the drought to end

although you know everything
there is to know
about the guile and the gristle
of the heart—
its handloom desires,
                 its spandex fantasies,
its polycot, its wear-and-tear
polytheism.

And you know
that when it happens again,

the whoosh

of textile, versatile,
block-printed by sun,

it will feel big enough
to put an end
to all the throbbing questions forever.

But the winters—
they get colder each time.

And so you return
reluctantly

to digging
through the stretch
and seam and protest
of tattered muscle,

deeper
into the world's
oldest fabric,
deeper
into the
darkening
widening
meritocracy

of the heart.

Clothed in Emptiness
Sri Annapurani Amma

A great raging river of a human being.

That was the image that first came to my mind when I met Annapurani Amma. A river in spate. A river that has foamed over its banks, uncontained by boundaries, unconcerned about limits.

A wildflower, said my traveling companion. The kind that you might miss entirely if you never walked aimlessly down a country lane. But when you do stumble on her— feral, inimitably herself—you can't help thinking of how impoverished your life would have been if you'd missed her. (She is no shrinking violet, though. Annapurani Amma has too much sass to be that kind of flower.)

Both images make sense to me: river and wildflower. Annapurani Amma is a character you could never dream up. She is an original. Her voice is loud and penetrating, her laughter near-hysterical, her hair a rainforest of matted wilderness. She seems the quintessential avadhuta. A reminder of what it means to confront life untamed, no holds barred. A life clothed in nothing but emptiness—open to a gasp of sky, a blast of ether. She is a reminder of what the word "digambara"—sky-clad—might *truly* mean.

Physically, she is stark naked. But as I look at her, seated majestically on her couch, I realize I am face to face with a woman whose face is, quite simply, her heart. There is no time lag here, no interval, no stepping stone between the human being within and without. Annapurani Amma is clad in nothing but herself.

In January 2017, I was visiting the temples of Kanchipuram with three fellow pilgrims. One idly happened to mention a "female saint" who lived in the vicinity. She ferreted out a video clip on her cellphone. A disconcerting figure emerged.

With her matted locks and rolling eyes, this saint seemed decidedly deranged. I suggested giving her a miss. We had tons of temples to visit that day. Kanchipuram was inexhaustible. Another time, I urged.

But my companion persisted. "Let's give it a try," she said.

We both knew what that meant. We were weathered-enough pilgrims to know that a meeting with a saint (if indeed she was one) required the hand of providence. It could not be orchestrated.

Some hours later, we found ourselves at the gates of an ashram in the village of Chinnalambadi. We were in the town of Uthiramerur, some eighty kilometers from Chennai. A Tamil signboard on the gates clearly informed us that Annapurani Amma met visitors only on weekends.

"So that's that," I said, turning away, relieved.

We had reached our car when a young man emerged, clad in a sanyasi's ocher. He greeted us politely and asked if he could help. My companion explained. He pointed to the signboard. Yes, we knew it was a weekday, she said, but we had come a long way, hoping for a darshan.

He looked at us, silently and appraisingly. "Wait here," he said and vanished between the gates.

We waited, the afternoon heat seeping slowly into our skins. And yet, there was a frisson in the air. Something unmistakable. An atmospheric cue. In the heavy silence of a late winter afternoon in the Tamil countryside, there was a moment of latency. The feeling of having stepped into a field of possibility, when the goldfish bowl of your life suddenly widens into a larger orbit, a bigger plot. A threshold moment.

The brahmachari returned. "She will see you," he said quietly.

We were not surprised. A sense of inevitability had begun to take over. The afternoon turned suddenly dreamlike, alive and unreal all at once.

As we entered, the brahmachari told us that we were at the site of a Brahma Peedham, a memorial to the legendary eighteenth-century Tamil saint, Sadashiva Brahmendra. We followed him past the granite visages of south Indian yogis and saints from Agastya to Karuvurar. He led us past a Muruga temple into a large hall, the site of the memorial.

I didn't hear what he murmured before opening the doors. It was (I guessed later) about the fact that his guru did not wear clothes, except when she held public gatherings, satsanghs, on weekends. Since I heard nothing, I entered the hall unprepared.

Annapurani Amma sat before us on a couch. A woman with the presence of a lion. And a body as smooth and tawny as the great beast of which she was reminiscent. She wore her nakedness casually, her body a garment she wrapped almost abstractedly around herself.

She welcomed us with an imperious expansiveness. She invited us to sit before her, and told us she had consulted her guru about whether to meet us. "He said, it's all right, call them in, and so I did," she said, her eyes gleaming, her voice resonant with laughter.

Her guru, we learn, is none other than Sadashiva Brahmendra, the naked saint and advaitin mystic of Tamil Nadu, whose compositions still suffuse the repertoire of Carnatic musicians. I grew up with the strains of "Manasa sancharare" (Mind, journey toward the Supreme) and "Pibare Rama rasam" (Drink the essence of Rama) in my ears, thanks to parents whose love of classical music pervaded my home. I had visited his samadhi in the little village of Nerur some years ago. It was enveloped by that indefinable hush—the kind that surrounds places with extraordinary energy fields. I called it the feeling of being drenched with nimboo-soda, sparkling lemonade, on a summer day. The change in weather is unmistakable.

Sadashiva Brahmendra lived three centuries ago. But Annapurani Amma wears the centuries as casually as she wears her nakedness. Sadashiva Brahmendra is a living presence for her. More alive than any of us before her. Clearly many times more precious.

We sat with this woman for an hour that day.

I wrote a poem about her later. Verse seemed to be the only possible response after an encounter of this kind. Annapurani Amma didn't lend herself to prose.

In July 2018, I visit Annapurani Amma again. This time by design.

I have watched a couple of Tamil television interviews with her in the interim. She has a small local following, but news of her nakedness has obviously reached a few in the big city. She wears an ocher mundu around her torso in the interviews. Her manner is outspoken, her demeanor wild. She seems to revel in it. I can see one interviewer throw questions at her with a journalist's seasoned sneer. She does not respond to the irony. She continues playing the madwoman, delirious, loud-voiced, shrewish. It is clear that she doesn't mind being considered unbalanced.

I think of the many mystics down through the ages who actively cultivated such an image to keep out the idly inquisitive. Spiritual literature is replete with accounts of mystics who fiercely guarded their anonymity, and grew adept at speaking a veiled language, littered with red herrings. It is a smart ploy to ensure that only authentic seekers turn up—those who are so ravenous that they are willing to pick up crumbs of guidance from any source, however socially unacceptable.

The flamboyance and outrageousness seem, in fact, to be the unique selling point of the avadhuta—the holy fool, the wise lunatic. The figure abounds in traditions around the world, although the degrees of strangeness vary. This is not the joyless, law-abiding ascetic, but the ecstatic renunciate who has discovered the freedom of shaking off all cultural cargo—social decorum, religious propriety, worldly consideration, and sometimes even clothing. Plato termed the condition a gift from the gods. Variations on the theme range from Socrates and the Greek oracles to legions of shamans and mast Sufi mystics, from Jesus and St. Augustine to Zen mystics such as Ikkyu and Ryokan. Shakespeare's Fool clearly showed signs of such ancestry, as did Mulla Nasruddin, Birbal, Tenali Rama, and innumerable other trickster and shape-shifter archetypes.

Perhaps few countries can boast of the everydayness of this condition in quite the same way as the Indian subcontinent. For though it is difficult to tell the real McCoy from the counterfeit, there is no Indian who has not seen some version of the mad saint, at least somewhere at the periphery of their vision.

The earliest recorded avadhuta was probably Shiva, the untamable mystic of the upper Himalayas, who, when cajoled into marriage, asked in amusement, "Who? Me? What need have I of a wife?" And yet, the ash-smeared yogi and legendary outlaw seems to have plunged into the roles of husband and father with exuberance and passion, never losing the naturalness, the freedom, the intoxicated equipoise of one who sees through the game but is still unafraid of playing it. The sage Dattatreya, associated with the Natha yoga tradition and author of the medieval text the *Avadhuta Gita*, sings: "The avadhuta . . . living in the holy temple of nothingness, walks naked, knowing all to be Reality." Again, he exults: "Pure as space he walks, immersed in the immaculate bliss of his natural state."

The subcontinent has seen its celebrated women avadhutas as well. The twelfth-century naked ascetic Akka Mahadevi is widely known in southern India for her poetry of extraordinary richness and lyrical abandon. Her outpourings, which constitute some of the finest work of Kannada literature, offer glimpses of her wanderings through the countryside drenched in a state of exalted awakening. "I have Maya for mother-in-law, the world for father-in-law . . . / And I cannot cross the sister- in-law . . . / But I will / give this wench the slip / and go cuckold my husband with Hara, my Lord," she declares. Lal Ded, the fourteenth-century Kashmiri mystic, is another figure who stands tall in the collective consciousness of this land, as a woman adept who shrugged off oppressive family ties, worldly possessions, and clothing to walk the world alone. In a poem, she exclaims: "My Master gave me just one rule / Forget the outside, get to the inside of things. / I, Lalla, took that teaching to heart. / From that day, I've danced naked." Meerabai, ecstatic lover of Krishna, did not drop her clothes, but stripped off much else in her legendary quest for freedom. "People say / I'm mad / mother-in-law says / the ruin of our clan," she sings in what is now an immortal anthem to sacred depravity. Janabai, the thirteenth-century poet and maidservant in the home of the great Varkari saint Namdev, was empowered by the same lunacy to invite her personal god, Vitthala, to wash her hair and do the dishes in her jauntily irreverent verse. "I eat god, I drink god, I sleep on god," she says in poetry that displays a breathtakingly informal relationship with the divine.

A more recent example is the colorful twentieth-century south Indian mystic, Mayamma. Clad in rags, her hair unkempt, the wild woman of Kanyakumari was often seen laughing, wandering by the seashore, followed by a faithful pack of stray dogs. Believed to hail originally from Assam, Mayamma herself never spoke of her antecedents. She had no home, and was never heard to give any teaching. Whatever food came her way was shared with her dogs. Her behavior was bizarre by any standards, and yet, it became apparent to her townsfolk that this was no ordinary woman. Her very glance was considered miraculously healing, and her silence eloquent in its power. Over time, the seaside teashop owners began to pray for her to turn up at their door every morning. She would often snatch idlis from their trays and feed her dogs. But if she chose to grace their shop, they were guaranteed a day of booming business. If she so much as appeared in one's line of vision, it was considered a blessing.

There are countless undocumented figures of this kind. Indeed, the folk memory of every Indian hamlet still boasts of its homegrown avadhuta—one who took that terrifying leap into a life without labels and lived on to remind us that coming apart can sometimes mean coming home.

In her half-crazed manner and railing prophecies about tsunamis that might wipe out Chennai, I see that the media doesn't capture any of the vibrancy or complexity of Annapurani Amma. Online, she is a mere oracle, a somewhat hysterical soothsayer. She is not the fearless woman I had met a year ago, the woman who wore her body like a lion.

It is in quest of the lion woman that I set out in July.

As my car races past Chengalpattu, I think about the woman I am about to meet. I cannot vouch for Annapurani Amma's spiritual credentials. I am in no position to judge them. There is no way to experience someone else's interiority. But there are many ways, I believe, to sniff out realness.

I am with Annapurani Amma because she *smells* real to me. I don't really care whether her prophecies come true. I am not interested in her as a clairvoyant. I am interested in her as a woman on a path so real for her that it has empowered her to take sanyas, drop her clothes, and sit on her couch with a freedom that awes me. She may or may not possess the poetic genius of an Akka Mahadevi, or the legendary musicality of her famed guru, Sadashiva Brahmendra. But she has gumption. Oodles of it.

She welcomes me and my party of two with warmth. She is the way I remember her—vibrant, cackling, reckless, expansive. We spend four hours with her.

To recount those four hours in terms of a linear narrative is an impossibility. Annapurani Amma is nonlinear—in appearance, in manner, in conversational style. She invokes an incident in her life, then bursts into song, then leaps to the future, and dives back three centuries into the past with a whirlwind velocity.

I gain more coherence from her disciple, Ram, the quiet brahmachari who greeted us on our first visit. The biography of Annapurani Amma he offers is sketchy but offers a semblance of chronology.

She was born in 1967 in Chennai, he says, and moved to Tiruvannamalai soon after her birth, where she spent the first few years of her life. At the age of five, she had visions of the Goddess (whom she calls Navashakti Sengazhuneer Dattatreya Mariamman). The connection with Devi deepened rapidly. By the age of twenty-three, she was fully immersed in the spiritual life and had renounced ties with her family. In 2002, her guru, Sadashiva Brahmendra, appeared to her. After that, there was no looking back. She had found her path.

Ram met her in 2006. He was a young engineering student at the time. "I was searching for a male guru. I felt a tug when I read about Sadashiva Brahmendra in a book. And when I met Amma, and heard her narrate the life of the guru, the *Guru Charitram*, to me, I knew I had to be with her."

She was directed by her guru to take formal renunciation, or sanyas, from Sachidananda Swami of Kerala on January 3, 2004. The Swami bestowed the name "Premamayeema Mataji" on her. However, Annapurani Amma is the name by which she is known to her devotees. In 2010, she started living a life as a naked sadhu. Her hair began to grow matted. She built the memorial for her guru, Sri Sadashiva Brahmendra, with her personal resources (a meager thirteen lakh rupees), Ram tells us. Later, with her devotees' help, an ashram was built. She has so far conducted two consecration ceremonies (or kumbhabhishekhams) for the ashram—which she terms her guru's abode—in the years 2007 and 2017.

That is as linear as the story gets. When I try to cross-check facts and dates, they grow blurry. The contradictions mount. I give up. For a sense of the actual roller-coaster encounter, it is back to the mystic herself.

"This land is holy. Unimaginably holy," declares Annapurani Amma, her gaze moving rapidly across our faces.

She seems to be studying us, sizing us up. Her gaze is curiously personal and impersonal all at once. A dimple appears fleetingly in her cheek, reminding me that she must have been an attractive woman. There are photographs of her around the hall that depict her in her youth at the shrines of various saints. She is pretty, glossy-haired, in these. She is striking even today, but pretty is not the descriptor that she evokes. Indeed, she seems to be at pains to ensure that any idea of decorativeness is furthest from the mind.

I am fleetingly reminded of a novel of my childhood, and its figure of the "mad woman in the attic"—the archetype that women even today keep safely locked up. Unleashed from their psychological garrets, these energies can be decidedly unsettling for the world. And yet, one knows that the refusal to draw on these "attic" reserves can turn one into a limited version of oneself—often toothless, lifeless, insipid. Charlotte Brontë, that nineteenth-century creator of the mad woman of the attic, surely knew that too.

There is something exhilarating about this presence before us. For a naked woman sadhu, I realize, the "mad woman" demeanor is probably both liberating and convenient. It keeps at bay the spiritual tourists and curiosity hunters.

"Do you know my guru, Sadashiva Thatha?" she asks. We nod.

"He lived and meditated here for twenty-five years. Did you know that? How could it be anything but holy?" she asks rhetorically.

I am struck by the affection in her use of the epithet Thatha—grandfather—to describe her guru. Her voice softens when she invokes him.

"I have followed his instructions painstakingly to create this memorial," she says. "He told me exactly what to do, and I obeyed. Every word." Three centuries are evidently no barrier to this guru-disciple relationship.

"Few know this, but Thatha consciously merged with the infinite in *three* places," she continues. "That is, he took jeeva samadhi in three destinations. The first place, associated with his physical body (sthula sharira) is in Nerur. The second—with his subtle body (sukshma sharira)—is in Manamadurai. The third—associated with his causal body (karana sharira)—is in Karachi, in modern-day Pakistan"

We digest this information.

"But he's been gone for centuries. How did he become your guru?" I ask.

She turns to me. "He called me," she says. "He said, 'Come on, my child.' And so, I did."

She speaks in Tamil, but the words "come on, my child" are uttered in English. "He speaks to you in English?" I ask irrelevantly.

She laughs. "And why not? He does not belong only to this region. He belongs to the world. They say he left his causal body in Pakistan! A guru needs no language. A single glance is enough to communicate. Do you think he is not capable of speaking English if he chooses?"

The question is rhetorical. And unanswerable.

"What does a guru mean on the spiritual path?" I ask instead.

I realize this is the one subject Amma cannot have enough of. She dives into it. This is her element. She is a woman swimming in guru bhakti—the ancient delirium that assails disciples when speaking of their spiritual masters.

"The guru is the person you can never buy. His compassion is extraordinary. He won't change for you but he won't rest without transforming you. His business is to mirror you, to show you who you are. He has taken birth for this simple reason. Don't treat him as a visitor. Don't shop for gurus. Once you meet him, treat him as your very breath. Don't doubt him. Don't suspect him. He knows your every move, your every thought, your every plan. Whatever path or by-lane you take, he is there at the other end, waiting for you. You think your guru doesn't know you're here? Oh, he knows all right." She laughs wildly.

"The guru is a thief, really," she continues. "He's waiting to loot you, to rob you of your very being, your identity. But so what? What do you have that is really yours?

"And never forget how much he loves you. He waits for you eagerly. Like a dog, loyal, steadfast, committed to your liberation. That's how simple he is. Do you hear him, barking away? He is your dog; don't forget that. You are his master too!

"But he works only if you hold him as your very life breath. And once you do, you realize he is tireless. Even the gods in their temples need their sleep, but not the guru. Temple sanctums close at noon, but the guru works around the clock.

"Don't judge him by his appearance, his grand clothes or the absence of them, his success or the absence of it, his fancy lifestyle or the absence of it. You exist because of his compassion. He is the only one in the universe who is willing to take on your karma. No one else will.

"When my disciples ask me for guidance, I point them to Thatha. He is my guru, I tell them. Surrender to him. Surrender your all. He has never failed me. Once you have surrendered, you need not go in quest of him; he will come to meet you.

"But how to surrender completely to the guru, they ask. I tell them: it's simple. Just look at everyone as your guru! That's one strategy that will never fail. He'll never be able to get away. The master wears many disguises. Once you look through the disguises, you see him everywhere.

"But don't delay. When he opens the door for you, enter. Don't hesitate. Enter now! If the door shuts, you do not know when you will get the next opportunity. Perhaps in another yuga, another era.

"Everyone finds the guru baffling. Every day he wears a new form, a new garb. One day, he may travel in posh cars, wear silken garments. Another day, he discards all of it, and lives the life of a renunciate. One day, he is exuberant, and the next day, taciturn. Don't try to figure him out with your intellect. It will be futile. How does a mother know why her infant weeps? Not because of logic. She knows by instinct. Approach your path by instinct; you will recognize the guru effortlessly.

"Just remember: no deals are possible here. No agreements, no contracts, no guarantees. There is only love. And once you look at everyone with the gaze of love, you see every creature is divine. You start with clichés like 'the divine is love' and 'God is love,' and you end up with the realization that love is all there is. Love *is* divine. Nothing else matters. Nothing else *exists.*"

There are no dry eyes in this room. All of us seated before her have experienced, in our own ways, the transformative power of the guru. We sit with our own thoughts for a while.

At length, I change the subject. I ask her to talk about her personal life.

She starts obligingly with a list of biographical details, before veering off, characteristically, in another direction. "I am from Tiruvannamalai, but I was born in Chennai. Mine was a family of Dikshitar brahmins, a very conservative, very traditional Veda-reciting family. My parents were Rajagopalan and Shyamala. I was their second daughter. Later, after my sixth standard, we returned to Chennai again. We lived in the Tambaram Sanatorium, and I went to school there.

"The name of Rama was on my lips from an early age. I chanted it often. And the vision of the Goddess appeared to me at the age of five. This was the image of Devi with one half of her body as Shiva and the other half as Krishna.

She was wearing a long yellow skirt, a pavadai, with a red border. And I instantly became her slave. How could I not? Give up your ego, and realize yourself, she told me. So, the spiritual life started early."

I take this in, interested by yet another composite Hindu deity. I have personally never heard of this goddess, but I have no problem at all believing that someone else might have. I marvel at the great plural forest of the human psyche, and say a mental prayer that it is never tamed by a fundamentalist world—a world impoverished of imagination, terrified of multiplicity, suspicious of metaphor.

"I had other gifts that I never took much notice of. I could foresee things. People in difficulty began to approach me to predict the future for them. Later in my life, I knew that my parents would die in an accident. I told them that is how they would meet their end. I could see it clearly. And that is exactly how they did die, although it was many years later. They were hit by a lorry carrying sand for the construction of a Kali temple in Krishnagiri. Think of the irony of that—being killed by a truck bound for a Devi temple. The others in the car were saved: the driver, his wife, even their six-month-old baby. But they died instantly."

"Did you have a regular life at all?" I ask. "No worldly ambitions?"

Annapurani Amma cackles. "Of course I did. I wanted to be a lawyer. That was my earliest ambition"

We try to find out what turned an aspiring legal luminary

into a spiritual one. But it is not easy. Amma clearly does not wish to dwell on her past.

"I discontinued my studies after class ten; never went to college. The lawyer dream didn't work out. I married young (which was typical of my kind of traditional family), had two sons," she says briefly. "But when my children were just aged five and three, my guru called me. He said, 'Come on, my child.' And so, I did."

We are back to the summons of Sadashiva Brahmendra.

"I was different. Always different," she says suddenly, looking at me, as if reading the next question in my mind. "That's why none of this seemed strange to me. Wherever I met swamis and sages, they recognized that. One called me 'Meerabai.' Another spontaneously called me 'Radhe.' A third called me 'Patanjali.' But my guru only called me 'my child.'"

"Was the guidance of the goddess not enough for you?"

She smiles. "The goddess was magnificent. But she always told me, 'I am not the end of your quest.' I kept asking her, 'What is the end?' When I met my guru, I knew what she meant."

"You seem to have met many spiritual teachers. Didn't you think of any of them as your guru?"

"I searched feverishly for guidance. My parents were devotees of a holy man from a place called Kelambakkam, a Chennai suburb. He was called Gnanacheri Swamigal, or Kelambakkam Swami. I have visited him ever since my childhood. I remember wanting to ask him to give me his blessings so I could become a lawyer and drive my own car. But each time I entered his room, the only question that came to my lips was, 'When can I take sanyas? When will I become a renunciate?'

"It was strange. As soon as I left his room, the desire for a career in law would return. I would plan to tell him of my noble aspirations—how I wanted to amass millions in order to fight legal battles for the poor. But as soon as I entered his room again, the only question was about sanyas. Finally, I just gave up!

"But whenever I asked Kelambakkam Swami for sanyas, he would laugh and say, 'God will take care of it.' 'But aren't you divine? Don't you know?' I would demand. He only laughed. And there were a hundred shades of meaning in that laughter that I never understood then.

"He had a male disciple, Mahadeva Swami, who would never let any women stay in his room very long. That annoyed me. I would ask, 'Why are you allowed to remain here? Why won't you let women be in this space? Are women not allowed to lead lives of renunciation? One day, I will show you that I'm entitled to be here too.'

"I always tell people: Do not ask, 'Who am I?' All that intellectual self-enquiry is a waste of time. Change your question. Ask instead, 'Where is my guru?' That is the only question that counts. The *only* question that counts.

"So once when I asked Kelambakkam Swami this question, he replied, 'Your guru is not in his physical form. No embodied being in this world—and that includes me—is your guru.'

"It was then that I heard my guru's summons: 'Come on, my child.' The year was 2002. It was like a voice from the heavens. That beloved voice. I hear it even today. And so, the very next day, I went to Nerur. And there, I found my guru. My Sadashiva Thatha.

"The journey was challenging. I got onto a train to Nerur with five fellow seekers, all boys. I decided not to eat until I reached my destination. We were in an over-crowded compartment. Our seats were just near the toilet. I joked about it to my fellow passengers. 'My guru says, "Come, my child" and makes me sit right near the toilet!' I said. In just ten minutes, the entire compartment emptied out. Everyone else got off, and it was just the six of us the rest of the way. We could sit where we wanted.

"When we finally reached Nerur, everyone wanted a cup of tea. But the last bus to the shrine was announced just then, and we decided to forgo it. Nerur was a desolate place then— just a small hut, no food stalls, nothing. We got off the bus and thought we'd have a chai at the stall near the shrine, but there was some commotion there: the boiler had burst, and the tea and coffee had been spilled. We couldn't have any there ei-ther. It felt like my guru was safeguarding my pledge to go on an empty stomach to his samadhi!

"We went and met the priest at the samadhi shrine. He advised us to take a dip in the river and then come. So, we went to the river, the Kaveri. The boys went one way, and I went another. Although the priest had told me to have a bath, what he hadn't said was that there was no water in the river! It was dry. Dry as a desert. I grew tense. How was I to bathe in a river without water?

"I walked into the hot sand of the riverbed, wondering what on earth to do. And that is when I saw him for the first time. My guru. I mean, *physically*. He gave me a darshan in his actual physical form. He pointed me in the direction where I would find water. He climbed another mound of sand, and I walked with him. There was water there, and I bathed.

"After a bath, we entered the temple. The prayers had begun. We were served the prasadam, the holy offering, afterward and my heart's desire was fulfilled. I had fasted successfully. And my guru had led me to water. Who else could slake my thirst? If he had not come to me, I would never have come this far. He said, 'Come on, my child,' and I have been following him ever since.

"I have often longed to touch him. Often, I've wished he was in a physical form, not in a subtle body! That's when he instructed me to build this shrine. And so, I did. This is my way of touching him. Of making him *tangible*."

"How did your life change after meeting him?"

Amma clearly does not want to return to this chapter of her life. "My life changed completely," she says offhandedly. "In one month, I moved from riches to rags. He told me, 'I will take care of you.' And I trusted him.

"Mind you, it hasn't been easy. I have suffered hardships. I've lived in extreme isolation. When I first came here, it was in the middle of the wilderness. I've been called a prostitute. I've been called a madwoman. But eventually, he made sure I was able to sell my property for enough money—enough for me to give everyone a share, including my children. Even today, there is no donation box in this place. I have never had to beg. My guru has taken care of that. Offerings made in love and equanimity are accepted; not others. Thatha told me, 'I will take care of your children.' And today, my sons have grown up into self-reliant young men."

"Do they visit you?"

"Sometimes. But I don't give them any special treatment. I don't allow any of that glue of maternal affection to stick to me. They sit in the last row before me, just like any other devotee. They know that if my guru beckons, I will go like a shot. I won't look behind me to see who's following. I have built this ashram and this temple for my guru. But I'm willing to walk away even from this any time he calls me. That is my freedom.

"My sons sometimes complain. They tell some people here, 'You are free to touch my mother and speak to her, but we cannot even touch her!' It seems unfair to them. One of my sons laments, 'Why did Amma leave me? Why couldn't she be just a regular mother to me? Why am I deprived of the experience of a mother?' He came to me and asked me, 'What terrible deed have we committed to deserve this?'

"What can I say to them? Do they have it in them to understand me? No. They lack the maturity, the equanimity. But that is the way it is. I don't accept even a cup of coffee from their hands. This is the life of a sanyasi. They cannot walk in here whenever they feel like. They have to ask permission. If I am free, they can take my blessings and go. Otherwise not.

"And yet, when they go anywhere else to get the blessings of a holy person, they are introduced as the children of a wise woman, a gyani. It makes me happy to hear that."

"But wasn't it painful for you to give up your children, your home?"

"Painful? It was terrible," she laughs, her eyes filling with tears. "It broke me. People called me mad. People called me promiscuous. People called me all sorts of names. It is difficult for a woman to live like this—trying to protect your dignity, to take shelter in temples, to wander the world alone. There is no security for spiritual women in this world. Whatever you do, you are branded. If you wear rudraksha beads, they say you are putting on a fake costume. If you don't, they ask why you don't dress like a sanyasi. There's no pleasing them!

"Once when an interviewer came from a local TV channel to interview me, he asked me these questions. I turned around and asked him: And why exactly do you wear makeup? If a man can wear makeup, can't a woman take off her clothes if she chooses?

"My guru has protected me, always. He loves my dispassion, my fearlessness. I often question him. I've always been the questioning kind. I've never been afraid to point out mistakes, or to have mine pointed out. I tell my guru, 'If you have the right to do anything to me, don't I have the right at least to question you?' True renunciation is only possible when there is courage. Renunciation born of fear is not the real thing.

"When people called me mad, I went and told him about it. He told me, 'There are all kinds of people in the world, most of them mad about riches, position, power, family, attachments of various kinds. You are mad only about your guru. What's wrong with that?' That's when I realized there are varieties of insanity that are normalized by the world. We don't even notice these any more.

"Do you know what they did to my guru in his time, the people of this insane world? Do you know? Do you know what these 'normal' people did to him?" she demands fiercely.

This is a story I do know. It is legendary, this tale of Sadashiva Brahmendra, who in a yogic trance is said to have walked unknowingly past a king's harem. The king was incensed at the sight of a man among his wives, and commanded him to stop. When the sage did not heed him, the king's guards ran after him, drew their swords and severed his arm. But Sadashiva, in his altered state of consciousness, continued to walk, unmindful of the blood flowing from his terrible wound.

"He has seen it all, my guru. When he speaks of tolerance, he speaks from experience. He knew these men were going to cut off his hand. Still he allowed it. What can you say of such a master? He told me, 'When people abuse you, it reaches me, not you. It has nothing to do with you. Do not be troubled by it. I will handle it.' He put it so casually, so beautifully. Only a true guru can speak like this. Such is his love.

"I once asked Lord Shiva why he left me so alone in this world—so completely devoid of the support of a family. He consoled me. He said, 'The whole world is your family, dear one. You have more relatives than anyone else in the world.'"

I am struck by the casualness with which she speaks of Shiva. For Annapurani Amma, this is not a remote godhead, but yet another friend and companion.

"And then Shiva said, 'In any case, you will get a girl child named Valai Bala. She will call you her mother. You will never experience a moment's loneliness after that.' And that's exactly what happened." Amma laughs and gestures toward the young goddess idol to her left.

"Do you think she's pretty?" she asks me suddenly, as I turn to glance at the image.

I nod hesitantly. She looks like any other girl doll to me, large unblinking eyes and flowing skirt, but I know that is not the right answer.

"That's good. She likes to be praised. She's my daughter, Balakutty [Baby Bala]. She is only five years old. I need no other family now. I can ask for no more"

Later Ram tells us that the Brahma Peedham is dedicated

to the dual worship of Sadashiva Brahmendra and the Goddess, Valai Bala. Many childless couples who are referred by Amma to this goddess have been blessed with children, he says. She is the compassionate female principle who counterpoints the dispassionate guru energy of the place. "She is the only female deity worshipped by the Siddha saints of the south," explains Ram. "At times, Balakutty even speaks *through* Amma. It is amazing to watch."

I have watched the channeling in an online video, and am not sure I want to see Amma turn into a lisping girl child. Her current avatar seems formidable enough.

"What would be your advice to other women on the spiritual path?" my companion asks Amma.

Amma grins. "I would say just this: 'Foolish women, look at me.' Am I not proof that women can walk alone? That they can live on their own terms?

"There are only two kinds of people in the world: the strong and the weak. Someone asked me why I have so many male disciples. I said, isn't it self-evident? Because men need a mother. That is what I am to them. And there are other men who need wives. But women? They can take on the world on their own.

"Don't forget, Shakti, the feminine principle, is the basis of this universe. The foundation of it all. Think of all the women saints in this land: Karaikal Ammaiyar, Avvaiyar, Andal, Meera. Think of The Mother of Pondicherry. Think of Mayamma of Kanyakumari who walked naked. Aren't they evidence of women of courage?"

"And what made you drop your clothes?" I ask.

"And why not?" demands Amma. "There is no honor in wearing other people's clothes, is there? Every stitch on your body and everyone else's comes from someone else. Make no mistake about that.

"Many years ago, I borrowed my sister's sari without her permission. I did not think it a great offense. She was enraged when she found out. So enraged that she pulled it off me when I was returning from my office. In full public view! Today she denies ever doing such a thing. But I will never forget the humiliation of that moment. My self-respect was at stake in the middle of a street!

"What made it worse was that even my mother did not question my sister's behavior. That hurt me very deeply. My father used to be so particular about my appearance that he would even help me choose footwear that matched my clothes. But everything changed in a single moment! I did not speak to my parents after that until they died. I felt betrayed, broken, angry. I never forgave them for it. I kept quiet then, but that was also a lesson for me. I learned then that one must depend on no one. No one whosoever. I hope I have taught my children the same thing: do not depend on relatives. Ever. Learn to be independent."

As she speaks, she grows wild-eyed, distraught, crying. As I watch the avadhuta turn into a young woman again, I am struck by how deeply connected the divine is to human vulnerability. No layers of sedimented experience separate this woman from herself. She flows into all her roles all at once: child, woman, devotee, lover, guide. There is not a moment that seems inauthentic.

"But today? Today I am free. I am beyond humiliation," she says. "I have not come to spirituality in sadness. I have come in joy. My guru has taught me how to live in honor, in dignity, in renunciation, in self-respect. But I want the world to know what I have faced. It is not easy for a woman to transcend social barriers and walk the spiritual path alone. Every night, she is vulnerable, easy prey for the world.

"What kept me going? Just my guru, who told me, 'Your honor has gone. So what? Just think you are liberated from its clutches.' If he had not bestowed that equanimity on me, I would not be what I am today.

"I have taken off my clothes in full awareness. I left behind all attachment, so where was the need to wear clothes? There is not a trace of sexual desire in my body, so nothing about my presence induces lust in others.

"My sons are still disturbed by it. They ask, 'Why can our mother not wear clothes?' But I am no beggar, so why would I need clothes? I have a guru who has never allowed me to live as a beggar. When you take off all clothes, all false appearances, you have nothing more to lose. That is freedom. That is wealth.

"The vulgarity does not lie in taking off your clothes. It lies only in the gaze of the perceiver. Those whose vision is soiled see only sex wherever they look. If your gaze is filthy, my nakedness will be disgusting and shameful for you. Otherwise, not. It makes no difference to me. When you are naked in full awareness, nothing can touch you. My own guru walked the world naked. Why on earth shouldn't I?" Her eyes are blazing now.

We are silent.

"The mind is a monkey," she says. "You know Anjaneya, Hanuman, the god we call a monkey? The irony is he is not a monkey at all! The rest of us are. He is one-pointed. For him, there is only one name that counts: Rama. He is dispassion incarnate. It's the rest of us who are monkeys, and we don't even know it.

"I had lost everything by the age of twenty-three—my marriage, my children, my wealth, my property. Since then my life has been devoted to the spiritual. Formal sanyas happened later when I was directed by my guru to go to Sachidananda Swami of Kerala and ask him for it. But I had already left everything by then. The shame, the dishonor, the difficulty, the disgrace—I had already seen it all. Today, I have no family or social ties. I don't remember my earlier life. Nothing at all. Everything was a falsehood; everything was based on greed and wealth"

"Are you ever lonely?" I ask after a silence.

"When I had renounced my marital home and family, I wept and told my Lord Shiva that I had no one to look after me. I told him the world had abandoned me. He consoled me and said, 'Karuvurar, the great yogi, is your uncle, your chithappa (father's younger brother); Agastya, the sage, is your other uncle, your periappa (father's older brother);

and Shirdi Sai Baba, he's your secretary! What more do you want?'" She bursts into hysterical laughter.

We laugh uproariously too. We are not sure why.

I am not quite sure what to make of this capacity to shift unabashedly between the preposterous and the profound. Amma cannot be bullied because she is unafraid. She is unafraid because she has nothing to protect—no possessions, no relationships, no reputation. She is naked in every sense of the word. Here, I realize, is the formidable power of defenselessness.

"So, you talk to Shiva too?" I ask. "And to Karuvurar, Agastya and Sai Baba?"

"And to Muruga," she says casually, invoking the deity beloved of south India. "I didn't like him very much at first. I mean, he had two wives!" She looks at us to see if we share her indignation. I can only smile. Carried along by the tide of her narrative, I realize I have turned from interlocutor into listener.

"I didn't approve of that at all. Why should a man have two wives? Just because he's a god? But then, once the face of Muruga from a calendar spoke to me."

"A calendar image?"

"Yes. Straight from the calendar. He said, 'You are singing about everyone else. Why don't you sing about me too?'

"I said, 'Because you have two wives and I don't like you.'

"But he won me over. He said, 'You like the mother but not her son? You like Devi and not me? Is that fair?' And so, I gave in. Now, I sing songs to him all the time."

She bursts spontaneously into a song in praise of Muruga. Her voice is unfaltering, pitch-perfect.

"I now have a Muruga idol right here! I asked a sculptor to make it for me. He refused initially, but his son got a bit crazy and started shouting 'Muruga, Muruga' at home. The sculptor got worried. He thought his son was going mad. He finished the idol and delivered it in just seven days."

I am beginning to enjoy this woman's back-slapping familiarity with a pantheon of gods and saints. "And Shirdi Sai Baba?" I ask. I am particularly curious about this early twentieth-century mystic, now a pan-Indian figure, with a burgeoning tribe of devotees around the world. He has been a significant figure in my life, and I have made several journeys to his shrine in Shirdi in western India.

"Oh, I've met him, of course." Amma is as matter-of-fact as ever. "Met him in person. I call him 'Old Man.' I've held his hand, walked with him. I am not fond of these long-haired, unkempt babas. But one day when I was in Parangimalai (St. Thomas Mount in Chennai), my goddess told me to go sing a song at the Draupadi Amman temple. It was a Thursday, I remember. I did as she asked. There were several Sai Baba devotees there who stopped me.

"'Who are you to stop me?' I asked them. 'I'm here with orders from my mother, my Amma. I cannot stop.' But they insisted.

"I looked up and saw all these pictures of Shirdi Sai Baba, the object of their devotion. 'This one is a fraud,' I said to myself and left the place.

"But then he appeared to me in a bazaar! I still remember the scene. I was standing outside a shop—it was called Vijaya Priya Fancy Store, I remember. I was hunting for a skirt for my goddess when this old man of around eighty years with a white turban appeared and grabbed hold of my hand. He said, 'I like your music. I want it.'

"I thought he was nuts. I turned to the shop owner and asked, 'Can't you see this old man holding my hand?'

"The shopkeeper thought I was crazy. He said, 'See whom?' I realized then that no one could see what I could.

"'I am Baba, and I've come from Shirdi,' the old man said. 'You called me a fraud, right?'

"I couldn't believe it. I said, 'How come the shop owner can't see you?'

"'You want him to? Will you accept who I am if he does?' Baba asked.

"And the next moment, the shop owner asks, 'Who is that old man with a white turban beside you?'

"I didn't know what sense to make of this. 'I belong to my Devi,' I told him. 'You want me to change sides? No chance. I like only my goddess! And that's how it's going to be.'

"'But I like you,' he said.

"I was dumbfounded. What does one say to that?

"We talked for a while. He convinced me that just because there were people around him claiming to speak on his behalf, it didn't make him a fraud. I finally saw his point.

"We walked together. He even came home with me. Then he asked me to sing for him. I refused initially. Said I sang only for my goddess. But eventually, I did. After that, we talked at length. He gave me several words of encouragement for my spiritual journey.

"I have met him on other occasions too. In the Tambaram Sanatorium there is a recently built Sri Vibhooti Sai Baba temple. It was the fifteenth day after it had been installed. Sai Baba instructed me to go there and sing. I refused initially. But he arranged for my auto rickshaw to be punctured right outside his temple, so I had to get out and do what he asked! As I sang there, the ash kept pouring out of Baba's idol. My eyes were closed. But those who had gathered there were amazed. They took the shawl and garland from Baba's shoulders and placed them around me.

"My son happened to be there, and he cried out, 'My mother is divine!' He had always seen me as his mother, and never taken my spiritual life seriously. Now the old man taught him a lesson.

"Later, I told my guru, Sadashiva Thatha, 'Look at that old man, Shirdi Sai Baba. Look at the great air-conditioned marble temple his devotees have built for him. Why is there no shrine for you? Why are you sitting under a simple vilva [wood apple] tree?' So, he said, 'Okay, then build me one.' And so, I did."

We laugh again, together. Is all this for real? The question is irrelevant. It is real for Annapurani Amma, and she is real for me. For now, that is enough.

"And don't think I only talk to gods," she says suddenly, reprovingly. "I talk to others as well. The goddess teaches me Christian hymns too. I have composed songs for Jesus. Do you know Saint Anthony? He is a Christian saint. I sang a song for Saint Anthony in a church once.

"I love him because he is a true guru. If you light a candle or put a flower before him, he appears before you right away. I lit a candle before him once in a church, and he appeared before me. I asked him who he was. He said, 'Your guru.'

"I said, 'My guru? Sorry, my guru is someone else!'

"He said, 'You keep saying that your guru exists in everyone, right? I say the same. If your guru was here, what would he have asked you to do? He would have asked you to sing. So, sing!'

"I asked him if I should sing a song about him, and he said, 'Yes, sing.' So, I did." She pauses to sing a Tamil hymn to Saint Anthony.

"And I place flowers regularly for Hassan and Hussain as well. The guru tradition has no religion, no caste, no language. There are no differences here. We have a Muslim who comes here and adorns the idol of Hanuman with a betel-leaf garland. So what? This tradition never divides on the basis of faith. And nor do I. My heart is open. Open to all faiths, all traditions."

"So, what is the fundamental teaching you offer your disciples?" I ask.

"That the guru and God are one," she says simply.

"Nothing more. I am a scripturally uneducated woman, I have never been to a living guru. The only guru I consider to be mine is Sadashiva Brahmendra. I know no other. I don't set aside special hours for meditation for the disciples who live here. There are no dietary restrictions, no taboos against eating onion and garlic. I tell them, keep doing whatever you have to do with the guru on your mind. That is real dhyana, meditation.

"That's been my path. I haven't done anything. I'm a dunce. Never studied any book. The instructions on what to do—the mantras, how to conduct the rites, the poojas, at night—all of them come from Thatha. I don't tell my students to renounce the world, as I did. And I don't tell them to meditate. I tell them: just learn *to live meditatively*.

"Simply tuning out the world, closing one's eyes is not meditation. You should be able to meditate outdoors, my guru told me. I tell people: learn to be meditative with the tape recorder blaring, the television on at full volume, the fan whirring, the children running around noisily, family battles in full swing. Now sit and meditate, if you can. If you're able to manage it, this is true meditation. Don't think it's going to be all quiet and peaceful in the forests. Those who did penance in the wild know that you encounter bird noises, animal noises, insect noises, hunting noises out there. The forest is not a peaceful place at all!

"So, I tell people who come here, 'The only question that counts is, "Where is my guru?" Once you find him, nothing more is necessary. You have come home. You need no pranayama, no yoga, no ritual. Just trust him and follow him.'"

"You mean, follow 'her' in this case," I interject.

"No. No, I don't." She is emphatic. "When devotees come to me, I direct them to Thatha. I say, he's your grandfather too. I have not come here with any mission to transform anyone. I have come here to work on myself. Some people have given me the title 'guru.' But for me, there is only one guru around here, and that's Thatha. I make sure he is at the forefront of everything. If people are searching for a guru, I tell them, 'Pray to Thatha; he will direct you to your master.'

"You know, when I talk about my guru, there is no fatigue. Only if I speak of other matters, I grow tired. We have no groceries in the ashram now, no grains. But I am not tense. I am not stressed. How can I be, when I have my guru here, sitting here, talking to me all the time, guiding me? I have never gone and asked him for anything. And he always provides, so there has been no need to ask.

"Take a look at my disciple here." She points to the ascetic, Ram, who stands silently in the corner. Ram smiles. "One day, he said he wanted a pomegranate. I wondered if he was trying to test my spiritual powers. I told Thatha, 'If you don't give him one, I will be humiliated. And what are you going to do? We don't have the money to buy any.'

"But Thatha assured me, 'Don't worry. One dozen will come your way.'

"And that's exactly what happened. I suddenly got a

telephone call from someone, telling me that I was going to have a visitor. I didn't want visitors that day, but the person was insistent. So, a lady came bearing a very costly basket of fruit! And, of course, there were twelve pomegranates in there. I smiled and said, 'My guru has saved me.'

"Thankfully, my disciple has not asked me for anything else since then! But now if he did, I would say to him, 'Go to Thatha; you will get what you ask for.'

"You know what the problem is? The problem is most people have a formal 'Madam-Sir' relationship with the divine. You need to *own* the guru. He is *yours*. He belongs to you. He's the only person you have the right to demand anything of. He's the only person you can share your entire life story with. But that is only if you approach him the way you approach your grandfather! With intimacy. With the same sense of entitlement."

I think of the poem by the Kannada saint Basavanna: "Don't make me hear all day / 'Whose man, whose man, whose man is this?' . . . / Let me hear, 'This man is mine, mine / this man is mine' / O lord of the meeting rivers, / make me feel I'm a son / of the house." And the great mystic of Dehu, Tukaram: "So far, O Hari, you have cheated millions at this game / But . . . I won't let you escape . . . / Now I am going to square with you." And the mystic of Maharashtra, Namdev whose intimacy permits him to hurl cuss words at his beloved god: "You have no pedigree / You are casteless! You are a thief! . . . the son of a whore!" Amma is testimony to the ways in which that legacy of seeing the divine not as boss, but as buddy, endures even today.

"No more questions?" asks Amma when I finally turn off my recorder.

I am silent. My head is a blur of tales and songs, thrumming with this wild, high-voltage presence before me. I might come back again if I find I have more questions, I tell her. Right now, I cannot think of any.

"Oh, you will return, will you?" she cackles. "Just remember: I may visit you too. You won't be able to imagine how and when. I do whatever my guru tells me. And the ways of Thatha," she adds mysteriously, "are inscrutable."

We leave the ashram, our heads swirling with this glimpse of an extraordinary intimacy—an intimacy between a master and disciple who refuse to be separated by time or place. Who see time as no barrier, and space as no impediment. Who see the body as a disguise, a mere costume—gossamer-thin, flimsy.

Just one more veil by which we obscure the wild nakedness of love from ourselves.

The Lover

The woman doesn't call herself
a saint,

just a lover
of a saint

who's been dead three hundred years.

She doesn't see people
on weekdays

but her master tells her
we're safe,

so she calls us in to where she sits,
her body blazing
in its nakedness,
            a crumpled afterthought,

its tummyfold and breastsag
and wild spiraling nipple reminding us that life
is circles—
crazy, looping, involuting, dazzling
circles.

She tells us
the world calls her a whore.

She told her master about it too
but he only said,

"The rest of the world serves
many masters—
family, money, lovers, bosses,
fame, power, money, money,
in endless carousels—

        the crazy autopilot
        of samsara.

But you, love, think only of me.
Who's the whore here?"

Outside the window
the sun is a red silk lampshade

over a great soiled bedspread
ricocheting in the wind.

Memo II

To choose
 the right table,

the right quarrel,
 the right gaze.

Not the conference
 of hungry eyes,
but the fellowship
 of those who stand aslant,

multilingual,
 listening,

their shadows
 four-footed, their wisdom

angostura, their hearts
 green sun and groundwater.

Those who hope to cut through the fog,
 uncurdle the dream,

but still weep
        unoriginally

for the moon.

The Reluctant Guru
Balarishi Vishwashirasini

Deep into the palm-fringed road from Coimbatore to Palakkad is a leafy lane, suffused with sleepy morning breezes. It leads to a hermitage that seems almost deserted. There is no bustle. No zealous smiles of recently converted acolytes here. No practiced namaskars of long-standing devotees. No reception counters. No security guards.

It is here that Balarishi Vishwashirasini lives.

When I first met her, I summed her up in my head with a single phrase: "all lit up from inside." It is an impression that has endured.

Our very first meeting was at a conclave of Indian spiritual teachers in Delhi (a Guru Sangamam, as it was called). I was introduced to her by the Tamil scholar and writer "Marabin Maindan" Muthaiah.

A small, poised young woman, she smiled her luminous smile at me and said, "So you've started your writing about

spirituality, have you?" The familiarity of her address surprised me.

We talked briefly and she invited me to visit her ashram
on the outskirts of Coimbatore. I promised to drop in.

Two years later, I did.

Balarishi talked freely. There was laughter in her eyes.
A knowingness.

I wanted to take notes of our conversation, but never
did. What I do remember is an invigorating couple of
hours. Sharply intelligent, articulate, unpretentious, her
sense of humor and air of composure left an abiding impression.

She answered my questions readily and graciously,
talking at length of her ability to access the deeper truths
of existence through nada or primordial sound. I told her I
was fascinated, as a lover of poetry, by the texture and
flavor of words, their shape, their grain. The fact that she
prioritized sound over meaning interested me. Above all, it
was clear that she was a seasoned explorer of places beyond the domain of sound—the realms of silence, the very
source and octane of language.

The mystic science of sound, nada yoga, is one of antiq-
uity. I have heard about it from my guru who has shared
his own explosive firsthand experience of the universe as
sound when he was at the Himalayan lake Kanti Sarovar.
There are resonances in every mystical tradition—from
the much-quoted lines of the St. John Gospel ("In the beginning was the Word, and the Word was with God, and

the Word was God") to the Sufi notion of Saut-i Sarmad, or abstract sound.

The poet Rumi's verse has its oft-quoted lines: "If someone doesn't want to hear / the song of the reed flute, / it's best to cut conversation / short, say good-bye, and leave." And "Quietness is the surest sign / that you've died. / Your old life was a frantic running / from silence." "Before its incarnation the soul is sound," said the twentieth-century Sufi teacher and musician Hazrat Inayat Khan. "It is for this reason that we love sound." And so, for the Sufis, the spiritual journey can be seen as a pilgrimage from tongue to larynx to the deepest cave of the human heart.

There is the Buddha's evocative exposition on "the subdued murmur of the seatide setting inward" that "brings liberation and peace to all sentient beings" in the *Shurangama Sutra*. There is also the beauty of the Australian Aboriginal creation myth that tells us the world was birthed in song, a worldview that makes us denizens of a sonic cosmos—a melodic eruption of land and sky, mapped in lyriclines and versetracks.

For the nada yogi, creation is a wilderness of pulsation, a spangled web of vibration. As scholar-poet Mani Rao says in her book *Living Mantra*, the Vedas and Tantras see "mantras as cosmic emanations, divine revelations or a priori forms." For the mystic seer or listener, these emanations are perceivable. This enables the guru to offer a carefully curated cluster of syllables—an aural thread to guide disciples on their homeward journey. Nada yoga becomes, then, a deepening treasure hunt from physical sound through subtler mental and psychic dimensions to the very source itself—para nada, nonvibratory sound, the stillness at the core of all reverberation.

It clearly has its therapeutic properties as well. I remember my fascinating encounter with a British shaman in London in 2011. A natural nada yogini, Judith Seelig spoke to me of how she had possessed the ability from her childhood to hear the language of plants. Hers was a fascinating siddhi, a mystic gift—an effortless sensitivity to an idiom of sunlight and leafsong. She told me how, as a young mother, she intuitively knew how to treat her children's ailments with herbs from her garden. It was only in conversation with other mothers that she realized that she inhabited "chat rooms" that others had no clue of. Still later, after several spontaneous mystical experiences (including a somewhat inconvenient one in a supermarket), she came into her own as a spiritual guide. She now harnessed her capacity to use vocals and wordless sound to help others access deeper, unacknowledged and often unhealed parts of their psyches. It is the work she is engaged in even today. "We seem to have become a species mostly attracted to self-promoters and trumpeters," she says, and I wonder at the impact of high-decibel self-promotion on someone with her preternatural level of sound sensitivity! Undeterred, Judith works in her unassuming and determined way at empowering individuals and groups to find themselves—work that she describes as part of an ongoing "song of love."

That afternoon, Balarishi spoke to me of truths that could not be addressed by the mind alone. She spoke of the guidance that came to her through unexpected quarters—through both sound and fire. And yet, she was far from anti-intellectual. She did not lament the lack of faith in today's barrenly scientific world. Instead, she emphasized the need for both heart and mind while navigating inner and outer journeys.

I remember her saying that although she'd started an ashram, she did not want to turn into a mere administrator, trapped in a creation of her own making. She was keen on retaining her freedom. The candor of that admission stayed with me. I knew I was in the presence of an unusual woman—one with an inner calling so compelling that she had been able to craft her life in accordance with it. And this had been achieved with a grace and maturity beyond her years.

As the meeting drew to a close, she spoke of Shiva—not as deity, but as guru. "Gurus are very compassionate," she said. "When your spirituality is without intention, they are with you. When your seeking is motiveless, they are with you. As for Shiva," she paused, and her voice trailed away.

I waited. I knew she was not talking about a philosophical abstraction. This was a personal experience—deeply felt, damply real.

"He is a giver like none other," she said. "Just a little authentic feeling from your side receives so much support from his. You have no idea how much. He blesses even the limited ego self, caught up on emotional and karmic levels. Such compassion."

That was when I knew I needed to return to meet this woman. The moment reminded of the way I felt during my early encounters with my own guru—the sense of being famished with curiosity. I knew I had to learn more about Balarishi and the state of equipoise that emanated from her. A year later, with the phrase "such compassion" still resonant in my ears, I visited her again.

Muthaiah told me Balarishi had invited me to a Guru Pooja homa, a powerful ritual with the sacred fire, in her ashram. This was conducted annually in December, he said, and was an opportunity to see Balarishi do what she did best: chant. I was glad to accept the invitation. With Balarishi, I knew a homa would not be mere tokenism, a hollow ecclesiastical exercise. The idea of offering sound to the divine appealed to me. I like the idea of the spoken word as libation—a sensual and aromatic gift to the gods. I believe the approach could make all the difference even to a modern-day public poetry reading.

I was not disappointed. What I witnessed was a high priestess at work, supremely self-contained, autonomous. Here was a virtuoso, her attention focused resolutely inward, as an exuberance of sound, a riot of tones, poured forth. There were flashes of familiarity in this whirlwind of velocity and rushing air—I thought I discerned Tamil here, Sanskrit there. But what I remember, above all, from that day is a voice that zigzagged between gravity and starsong. We sat in silence for hours, drinking in that kinetic flurry, the shimmer and dissolve of radiant sound.

I was struck by the way these mantras flowed from this small figure, as she stood, hands on hips, eyes closed, unfaltering. Her disciples (including her mother and elder sisters) stood around her, willing apprentices, waiting to be instructed. When we left, our energies were high, our heads buzzing with shuddering cascades of rhythm.

In February 2018, I visited Balarishi out of a compulsion I could not name. It was a strong inner prompting. I texted her and asked for a meeting. Her response was immediate. She said she had been expecting me.

When I met her, she explained this. During her meditations that day, she said, my face had emerged clearly in her mind's eye. "I was not surprised when you texted," she said.

In the spiritual world of seekers and gurus, Balarishi presents an anomaly. For one, she became a guru without ever being a seeker. The seeking, oddly enough, started *afterward*—a seeking for a way to relate her mystical calling with her own unfolding personality and self-understanding. Secondly, and even more interestingly, she is a reluctant guru. A guru trying to figure out how to respond to the inner summons that disrupted and redefined her life.

Balarishi is a guru-in-waiting. A teacher in formation. She is in the wings because she chooses not to be center stage—at least not on anyone else's terms. That makes this a particularly interesting time for me to be meeting her. I am curious to see the direction in which her life unfolds. She is full of surprises, and seeing the dexterity and confidence with which she walks her homegrown path, I know there will be more surprises in the years to come.

As I listen to her unravel her life story, I know I am fortunate to have met her at this point in her life when she is not merely accessible but capable of both reflection and vulnerability. She is a woman who still speaks of herself as process, not product, who hasn't yet allowed image to obscure her reality as a mystic. I am struck by her unvarnished honesty, her unwillingness to conceal her doubts.

Like so many, I have often felt uneasy about the growing marketing pitch that pervades the spiritual life. With the vast institutional support that bolsters organized faiths, perhaps a measure of self-assertion and marketing is the only way for the decentralized wisdom traditions of this country to make their presence felt. I do see that. And yet, I wonder sometimes if the low-profile sage exists any more, or is a defunct breed. Perhaps it is an outdated romantic notion?

At this moment, with Balarishi, it is different. She is at the start of a journey. She has been a spiritual child prodigy. A precocious child-mystic. A junior "life coach" before the term became glamorous. A spiritual equivalent of a circus performer. And now she is at the point of paring down identities that no longer have any value. She is a guide who knows her vocation but is not invested yet in image. She has answers, but she also has questions. She is not afraid to talk about both. This is the woman mystic in all her molten latency. In all her nascent about-to-happenness.

It feels like being present at the birth of a new story.

"How did this happen: this ashram, your life as a young rishi, Shiva? Do you ever wonder how you got here?"

I have various questions on the sheet in front of me, but I am not looking at them just yet.

She smiles. She does not brush the questions aside.

She looks at me consideringly.

"I feel very normal in many ways," she says at length. "But I cannot relate to identities like 'homemaker' or 'entrepreneur.' Or even 'guru' for that matter. And when I am in the middle of an intense spiritual experience, a so-called normal life is not my priority at all. It seems unnecessary, irrelevant."

"What kind of spiritual experience?"

"The experience of being one with Shiva," she says simply.

The morning air is crisp. I can hear a koel call in the tree above her. The pause is long.

"In that state of oneness, there is no 'I' and no 'you,'" Balarishi says. "There is no physicality. No mind, no thought. The individual does not exist. There is the realm of experience, and then there are glimpses of a dimension beyond experience. That cannot be put into words. At that moment, I ask for nothing more. That's why I always tell my disciples: be with Shiva for the sake of being with Shiva. Otherwise you limit the experience."

"And what happens when you descend from such an experience?"

"It is interesting," she replies with a smile. "When I come out of the experience, I witness the play of my body-mind. And I know it is important to keep a balance between this outer play and that inner experience. But I have learned to trust Shiva. I cannot trust my thoughts and impulses in the same way, because individuality is not always so reliable."

"And Shiva is always reliable?"

"Always," she says quietly. "Of course, he knows how to play around with his seekers! But you learn to enjoy it. You get addicted to him. Obsessed. When he's not playing around, you miss it." Her gaze turns distant. "I was in Varanasi recently, and I realized all over again that he's the focal point of my life and that is how it will always be."

So, who *is* Shiva?

She laughs. For me to understand she must rewind. I have no problem with that. I am in the mood for a story.

"I was born in 1984, the youngest in the family, a naughty child. I grew up near Vadavalli in Coimbatore. I lived with my parents and two older sisters. My mother was a multifaceted woman, an entrepreneur, an administrator, who ran a business successfully. My father was a more complicated person. He grew insecure, possessive.

Over time, he wanted to take shortcuts. That landed us eventually in a financial crisis.

"I was always a naughty child. But I awoke to my spiritual life at the age of ten. It was around my birthday [October 1] that I started receiving mantras. It was confusing. I began to hear snatches of what seemed like ancient Tamil literary conversations. It felt like I was eavesdropping on sages talking to each other. There were visuals too . . . of another time, another era.

"I didn't take any of it very seriously. But things started changing. Watching my father meditate, I decided to start meditating too. That's when I began to hear words crystallizing into mantras. Once when my family was traveling toward Theni, near Suruli Hills, to meet a local swamiji, I found myself writing mantras in old Tamil on the way. Something was definitely changing.

"Gradually, my parents started looking at me differently. It was clear to them that I knew something that they did not. One day they asked me if I could predict what would happen to their business. I found myself replying effortlessly. I said that they would lose everything and then gain it all over again. The words flowed out of me spontaneously.

"And that is exactly what happened. They *did* lose everything.

"When the last of their creditors came and took our television set, we were left with nothing. Around this time, we had to leave home because of the financial mess we were in. We started spending time in relatives' homes. My parents had their own personal issues as well, which made it a tense domestic situation.

"At the same time, my experiences were intensifying. In school, my teachers were more and more confused about how to handle me. I was able to see certain things more clearly than they could, and I was naughty enough to manipulate situations for my own ends. I definitely wasn't an easy student to have around!" she laughs.

"So, you were being seen as a spiritual guide before you actually saw yourself as one?"

She smiles. "It happened rapidly. Soon after this, I gave my first interview to a Tamil publication. The answers flowed out of me effortlessly once more. A couple of months later, an article appeared in the well-known Tamil daily *Dinamalar*. Now people started queuing up outside my door. It became difficult to go to school. I tried doing my sixth standard in a different school, but didn't study very much. It was impossible. The crowds in our home were increasing daily. My education came to an end. I later ended up taking my tenth and twelfth standard examinations privately."

"What kind of guidance could an eleven-year-old possibly offer?" I ask wonderingly.

"The answers were always there. And through the upheaval in my home life, I was able to guide those who came to me. I *learned* a lot too—reading their karmic histories, reading their body language.

"And internally, the mantras continued to flow, gradually turning from syllables to words in Tamil and Sanskrit, often in the rhythm of a Vedic chant. I did not know what to make of them. I didn't take my chanting very seriously. It seemed more like a hobby than anything else."

"How did you manage without any external guidance? Wasn't it unsettling—especially for a child?"

"It was an intense time. A time of inner cleansing. On the one hand, there were deepening spiritual experiences. On the other hand, there were the karmic challenges of a difficult family life. But I did receive guidance in my dreams. The ancient sage Kakabujandar and his wife Bakula Devi appeared to me regularly. Have you heard of them?"

I have heard the name of the Siddha saint of Tamil Nadu. I later read up on him. Evidently a major figure in the Siddha mystical tradition of southern India, Kakabujandar is believed to have lived around the seventh century, although the legend is that he has lived through the dissolution of the universe several times over, enduring through the cycles of destruction in the form of a crow (the Tamil word for which is *kaka*). He is regarded as first preceptor of the cosmos, instructing and clarifying the doubts of gods and all living beings down the ages.

"They were my first spirit guides," she continues. "It felt like I had always known them. They treated me like their grandchild. I would cry to them, complain about how I wanted more time to play but how I was being denied. They were very kind. They would humor me, console me. They helped me enormously through these difficult times. Today, Shiva is my all. But at this early stage, Kakabujandar was my greatest spiritual strength."

"What did he look like?" I ask curiously.

"He appeared to me as a body of light," she replies. After a pause, she adds, "But not anymore. It is not necessary now. He is one with me."

"Your parents, were they worried about you losing out on your childhood?"

She smiles wryly.

"They were busy with their own difficulties. They started promoting my spiritual life mainly because they knew it would run the household.

"Gradually, people around started controlling me. There were people around my parents saying, 'She should be quiet, she shouldn't be playing so much.' That would put additional pressure on me. My parents suggested that I wear orange at the age of eleven, and so I did. It was not a personal choice.

"I do regret not having had a childhood. This is why a certain unexpressed childishness remains in me even today. As a child, I knew intuitively which devotees had brought me chocolates! I would ask to meet them first, before the others. This earned me the name KitKat Swami! It's ironic: after the age of fourteen, my love of chocolates fell away altogether."

We both laugh.

"And what about your adolescence? How did it feel to

be a guru when other girls your age obviously had other interests?"

Balarishi pauses and smiles. "At the age of thirteen or fourteen, I had my first crush. It lasted around three to four months. It was the usual pain of adolescent love. It ended up pushing me further toward my spiritual journey. Now, looking back, I realize it was a good thing. It was part of a maturing process. But at that time, it was hard."

We are quiet for a time, jointly reflecting, I imagine, on that disruptive phase in one's life.

"When I was with my disciples, there was no problem. I needed no coaching. I radiated energy. I was naturally comfortable meeting them, offering blessings. The irony was that internally an entire spiritual life was unfolding anyway, but externally my parents were trying to *make* me spiritual. This was the contradiction. The main source of pain.

"But there was a turning point when I was fourteen. I went with my parents and a group of devotees to Tiruvannamalai. It was during the festival of lights, Kartikeya Deepam.

"As I sat in the temple, the priest came up to me and asked me to chant. I was terrified. But I couldn't say no. I could feel the eyes of many people boring into me. I closed my eyes. When the energies of people next to me are high, when they are receptive, my chanting is smooth and spontaneous. But this was an unfamiliar situation. I didn't know who all these people around me in the temple were.

It was terrifying. I closed my eyes, hoping devotion would carry me through.

"And it did. I chanted for more than an hour. At first what poured out sounded to me like Sanskrit, but some priests later told me that it seemed like a language older than that. For me, it was just energy and nada, a mix of sound and syllable like never before.

"After this, everything changed. I knew now that I could chant even in public. And I knew that chanting was in some way a very important part of my spiritual calling. Since then, I always close my eyes when I chant. I went to Tiruvannamalai annually for several years after that. But now I don't have to. Every mantra I utter now is Arunachala. Every mantra I utter now is Shiva. Nothing more."

"What do you mean?" I ask, hoping to have the enigmatic Shiva trope unpacked some more.

"Earlier, I didn't understand Shiva. I would ridicule him. I would say he was nothing compared to the great sages and gurus of our culture. But that was before I understood him. When he made me sit in his temple and poured that deluge of energy and sound through me, I realized the truth: He *is* everything. There is nothing more. He is the ultimate guru."

We are silent for a time.

"What was happening in your external life?"

"By the time I was twelve, my parents separated. My mother and I got ourselves this place [the ashram] with the support of some devotees. It was deserted land then, absolutely quiet. Other than a few devotees who visited us, there was no one for me to play with. I was lonely.

"My mother was very insecure. She didn't want me to go to school. When I was thirteen, I told her that I really wanted to go. But she would ask me, 'Who will attend to the rituals, the poojas? Who will look after the spiritual needs of the ashram?' All my devotees were apprehensive too. What would happen if I gave up my spiritual life? So, to please them, I would wake early, do my poojas. After that, a devotee would pick me up and drop me to a private tuition center and later pick me up and drop me home.

"All this made me very angry. I was angry at the way in which my life was being controlled. I don't carry that anger any more now, but at that time it was intense."

Balarishi pauses. When she starts speaking again, it is clear she is choosing her words with some deliberateness. "Everyone makes mistakes and I can see now that my mother was at a very insecure moment in her life. She has since grown into a very broad-minded parent. She encourages me to go out and see the world. She encourages me to eat out when I feel like it, even to wear jeans when I want to! She no longer wants to control me. For her, I am her spiritual guide. She is into her own practices and those have deepened her. We share a deep connection. Even if our mother-daughter relationship ends, I know our spiritual connection never will.

"But those weren't easy times. I would be tired sometimes and resistant to my new role. When people touched my feet, my body would swell, grow inflamed. These were the effects of other people's energies on my system. I still hadn't learned how to deal with them. Then there were those who wanted me to tell their fortunes! I didn't want to do that. That had nothing to do with the spiritual journey. We were at cross purposes. We were talking different languages. It felt sometimes like I was teaching French, but people were lining up for English classes!" She laughs.

"There was a sharp disconnect between my inner and outer worlds. But I realize now how important all those experiences were. All of them helped bring clarity and balance into my life."

"How did you heal the disconnect?"

"By the age of seventeen or eighteen, I decided to take a break. I started giving a monthly darshan, instead of two and three times a week. That gave me more time. I started traveling on my own. That helped me become more confident.

"Other than my anger, I had my own insecurities. I was uncomfortable around intellectuals. Once I was confronted by some hostile people. They asked me questions about the meaning of certain words in Sanskrit. When I couldn't answer, they started taunting me. They asked me if I was trying to cheat others, if I was a hoax. Their hostility scared me. I started growing more silent.

"But as I began to spend more time with myself, I also grew more in tune with myself. I began to revisit places that were important to me. At the age of ten I had visited Suruli Hills with my parents, and I remembered that I had felt an immediate connection with the place.

"I went again with devotees at the age of twelve, and the connection deepened. I asked to be led to a cave there. Instinctively, I knew where it was. It felt like a past-life connection. It became my guru kshetra, my sacred space. I conducted my first homa with my disciples here. It was raining. I still remember the rain. Such a downpour! We didn't know whether it would be possible to conduct it in such weather. But at one point, I looked up, and the rain immediately stopped! And that had *nothing* to do with me. I am just an energy channel when I perform any sacred rite. It's just that the many gurus who have gone before us are very compassionate. When your spiritual practice is without any ulterior motive, they take care of you. They are one with you.

"At my ashram to this very day, we celebrate December 16 as the day of Guru Pooja. That was the day I reconnected with my guru center in Suruli Hills."

"What does the fire mean to you?"

"I know the fire is sacred," she said simply. "For me, my pooja is not Agama- or Veda-oriented. It is intuitive. As I start chanting, and putting wood in the fire, I can hear the fire and the mantra conversing."

She stops. The suspense mounts. I have the sudden sense of what it might mean to eavesdrop on a dialogue between the elements.

"It's an explosion of energy," she replies as if reading my thoughts. "When the chanting grows intense, the fire responds. It grows large. And suddenly, there is no 'I' left anymore. Individuality drops away."

"So, the fire is a guide?"

"It lights up my journey. It clears the way. It shows me the way to myself."

The birdcall has subsided. The afternoon heat is growing. The green hush intensifies.

"If Suruli Hills is your way of reconnecting with yourself, what about Varanasi?" I ask eventually. "You said Varanasi is significant to you as well."

"I discovered Varanasi at the age of twenty-one," she says. "I remember sitting at the Kashi Vishwanath temple during the mangal arati, the first ritual, at 3:00 a.m. My life was never the same again.

"I was going through difficult times. I had been longing for guidance. I felt bad that I didn't have an external guru, that I didn't know how to lead my life, that I had no clue what I ought to be doing. I wondered if I was in fact deceiving people. People who said I was cheating others didn't help. I was confused. Lost.

"So, as I sat at that arati, I had just one prayer to Shiva in my heart: 'Give me a place to sit and let me chant for you. If you don't make this happen for me, I will not set foot in your temple again. I would rather invoke you at home, in my ashram.'

"At the same time, one of my devotees had told the

priest about me. The priest now came up to me and asked me to come into the sanctum with him. I was overwhelmed when he placed a mat for me to sit on and asked me to chant. I closed my eyes, and the mantras began to pour out of me. When I reached the end, the priests spontaneously shouted, *'Har har Mahadev* [a traditional invocation to Shiva].' They asked me if I wanted to do the pooja afterward. So, I did. It was so intense, that experience. I broke down and wept at the end.

"It is not that I received answers that day. But from that moment onward, my questions dropped away entirely. It didn't matter to me anymore that I didn't have a guru. Intellectual questions didn't bother me."

I wonder whether to point out that it is an old and familiar story—a woman trying to be heard, or more accurately, trying to hear herself, in a world that is still, in many ways, the preserve of male voices. "Have you found a new way to deal with it?"

"When confronted by questions I cannot answer, I have learned to say, 'I don't know,' and simply offer the person a cup of coffee or tea!" Balarishi laughs. "It is not my role to satisfy people. I now realize that. I can only give them what I am capable of offering.

"I also began to realize that the sounds of the mantras that were pouring through me could be used for inner awakening. Until this time, I would guide devotees in close circles, conduct poojas and homas, but with strangers, I would clam up. Now a system began evolving. I realized the power of certain mantras, and began to explore their impact on the inner system."

"Have you ever looked for a living guru?" As a seeker, it still takes me time to understand her path. I know I would never have been able to navigate my way without an external guide—one who helped awaken me to my own inner guidance. It is so easy to be deluded on this journey with its psychological blocks, its existential terrors, its delusions, its invisible pockets of resistance, of frozen pain. And yet, it is clear that Balarishi's inner guidance has been powerful and purposeful; or else, her remarkably original path could never have been charted.

"Just before my Varanasi experience, I had encounters with two spiritual guides who helped strengthen my confidence in my journey," she reflects. "First, I met Swami Satyananda of the Bihar School of Yoga. It was just before his mahasamadhi [his final and conscious exit from his body]. When I told him of my mantra experiences, he told me that all the deeper spiritual practices are connected to sound. He was very happy to meet someone who had a mantra experience as the primary inner guidance. He encouraged me to walk my own path, follow my own direction.

"I spent a week in his ashram and had a long conversation with Swami Satsanghi there who urged me to deepen the link between the mantra and meditation. It made sense to me.

"I was also touched by the compassion of Swami

Dayananda. He was, as you know, an intellectual, a great Vedantic guru. I have a great deal of respect for Vedanta, but I am not a Vedantin. My path is through direct experience. And still I felt, intuitively, that I should meet him. His compassion moved me. When I told him I wasn't sure of what I was doing and that I wanted to give up holding satsanghs, he said, 'No, no, there is a reason why these experiences are happening to you. Don't give up your satsanghs.'

"He didn't understand my path. In fact, he even argued with my mother once about my mantra experience. She defended me hotly. He wasn't convinced, but he respected me as a spiritual person in my own right. He was very fond of me and invited me to visit his ashram. I was touched by his kindness.

"But after Varanasi, the longing for a living guru dropped away completely. I knew that I could trust my inner guidance. Like Suruli Hills, Varanasi became my guru peedham. I feel Shiva everywhere when I am in that city. I also began to realize that the meaning of the mantras is not the point. Language has its own limitations. The point is *sound*. I have now named my path that of nada kriya.

"Some time ago, I received a letter from the priest of an ancient temple somewhere in Tamil Nadu asking me for more information about 'Nada Rishi Kakabujandar.' The phrase hit me like a thunderbolt. I hadn't realized Kakabujandar, my old spirit guide, was a master of sound! So many different threads seemed to come together at that moment: the childhood guide of my dreams and my own quietly unfolding path of nada kriya. I realized it was all linked!

"It felt like a blessing from my early spiritual guide, Kakabujandar, and his consort, Bakula Devi, reminding me that my path was a continuation of their own. I have always felt there is a great connection between the mantra and breathing techniques of nada yoga and the Siddha yoga tradition of the south. I know I don't fit into any single tradition, but the Siddhas are omnipresent. They are among the most compassionate teachers in the world! Great blessings pour through from them all the time.

"The Tamil region is full of Siddha shrines and samadhis. These are extraordinary yogis who mastered the five elements. Though they practiced several common techniques, many of them walked their paths alone. Just place a picture of any one of them even today, light a lamp before it and ask sincerely for guidance. It will be given. Unfailingly."

A disciple places cups of tea before us. I sense that the young sage needs a pause. I think about my own fascination with the aural aspect of poetry that has led me to her. I think of my deepening questions: how to turn language from ornamentation into aliveness, from cultural acquisition into swanflight. And I think about the weave unfolding here—this strange fabric involving my curiosity, a modern-day nada yogini, and legendary Siddha masters of southern India. I take my time before my next question.

"Could you explain your path of mantra guidance? How does it work?"

"A mantra generates an energy in an individual that is good because it cleanses the aura and removes blockages. There are many subconscious imprints we carry. These are connected to our karmic process and biographical or astrological backgrounds. They cannot always be handled consciously or analytically. Mantras can help to cleanse us of much needless pain and suffering. Pain can be purifying, but it can also cloud awareness and make us lose clarity.

"As one progresses on the path, one needs more than prayer. This is where the chanting becomes so useful. The body and mind have their own power and place. You can use them to reach a point where you drop them. That is why the mantra is such a wonderful vehicle. It can transport you to a place where you have only a cosmic awareness—the sense of being one with divinity. You are now one with Shiva. Everything else becomes insignificant.

"The root mantras (moola mantras) that are imparted by gurus to disciples are more vowel-oriented than word-oriented. This is an initiation on a deeper level where language can be dispensed with. It takes time to touch a person on this level. This is why gurus take their time before offering such an initiation.

"The amazing thing about nada yoga is that you can be an illiterate but still touched by sound. After all, matter came into being through sound and light; it is just a denser aspect of the same energy. You don't need to be educated or have performed some advanced level of penance to make sound your ally. We are *all* gifted with a primal sensitivity to sound. This can become a vehicle to take us to deeper, subtler frequencies of energy.

. "When you are on a spiritual journey, a cleansing technique through sound is easier to hold on to. It is so simple, so effortless—such a flexible and compassionate method. The grace of Shiva is always with you when you practice it."

"Does it imply faith in a particular belief system?" I hesitate before asking the question. It is clear that there is nothing narrowly sectarian in the way she uses the word "Shiva." The question seems pointless.

"There is no religion here, no belief system." Balarishi shakes her head emphatically. "In fact, at the age of ten, I often told people I must have been a Muslim in an earlier life! Because I found myself so pulled to the sound of the Koran. In Dubai recently, when visiting my sister, I happened to be sitting in a mall. Suddenly, the sound of the chanting of the Koran began. It was so beautiful, so deep. I felt an instant connection. The path of nada kriya is completely unrelated to any particular faith."

"What about other paths: karma (action) or bhakti (devotion) yoga, for instance? Do you advocate a mix of nada yoga with other disciplines?"

"The mantra can be a wonderful tool, but cleansing can take place in many ways that cannot be ignored. A dynamic person needs more karma yoga. A person who is caught up with more gross desires needs some basic cleansing. There will be conflicts in his or her life if a mantra is offered too easily.

"An ashram should have space for mantra initiation and lots of karma yoga. I have seen fluctuating minds settle down beautifully with this. I always tell my disciples, 'If at the end of the day you feel heavy, you have not performed karma yoga. When it is done right, you always feel energized. That is true karma yoga. You can actually feel your inner conflicts subside.'

"Currently, my ashram is based mainly on the japa system or the repetition of certain sounds. I am not disturbing that in any way. But I know that my mystical life is meant to express itself primarily through the mantra. This has been revealed to me in my meditations. The significance of this nada yoga will be progressively revealed in the future. I know that.

"So, these days I initiate individuals into nontraditional mantras. I work intuitively in deciding what is meant for whom. For others, I offer just two or three syllables in a particular tone, which can trigger some energy. Initiations are still one-on-one. Perhaps more systematization will happen in the future. When people have already trained in yoga and pranayama, the initiation becomes that much smoother and easier.

"A mantra is like a string of seeds that guides you through the inner realms, stage by stage. It is a connection between guru and seeker. It bridges the divide between the two. This is why even if you don't see your guru for ten to fifteen years, you won't feel the distance. The guru always knows where you're at. The mantra is the link."

"You were a guru without ever being a seeker," I say. "But what happened once you found your path as a nada yogini? What changed?"

"I have been through two stages in my life as a guru," Balarishi says with a smile. "The first is of feeling very attached to my ashram, my temple, my disciples. I went through the ups and downs of that. With disciples, I expected results quickly, and when that didn't happen, I grew impatient. There is a detached way to love people. You have to understand their karmic process, understand the astrological variables at play. You have to allow their inner awareness to blossom and guide them. But as a teacher, you want them to evolve very soon. I could not bear it when they made mistakes! This was a painful stage. I needed to arrive at a certain inner balance.

"But in the last couple of years, things have changed. I see that they must go through their own life journeys. My role is to be there, to love them, and offer them whatever I have to offer. It will take them time to mature, and it is my role to guide them in a detached way."

I recall the way she talked to me wistfully of the daily grind of running an ashram at our previous meeting. I wonder how she deals with the trappings of being a guru. Does she find them burdensome?

"These past few years, I have been a free guru, not worrying or bothering about the structure of my life or my teaching," she replies slowly. "I still ask myself: Should I decide which way my life should go, or simply be quiet and allow things to flow?"

There is a pause.

"I am not sure," she says, almost talking to herself. "Things are unfolding so beautifully that I sometimes feel I should allow them to take their course. But at other times, I feel perhaps it is important to set up a vision, a vow, or sankalpa, so it is easier. It is probably time to bring more of a system into the ashram, make it more structured, more organized. And yet, the truth is that I am not good at sankalpas!"

She laughs, and I find myself laughing too at the ease with which she melts down barriers of political correctness. This is what makes it a pleasure to spend this morning here. There is the relief of being with someone who hasn't yet chosen her public face. Balarishi is not playing life coach, guru, oracle. Balarishi is not role-playing. Period.

"It is easier to surrender, to allow things to take their course. That has never failed me in my spiritual path. But surrender can be a cover-up for laziness. So, the ideal is to keep working and allow the divine to take care of the fruits of the process."

"Do you ever wish it had been different? Would it have been easier if you had had a regular childhood? If your spiritual experiences had started unfolding later in life?"

She shakes her head with some certainty. "No, no, it is a good thing that I started out at the age of ten. It would have taken even longer for me to arrive at this point had my spiritual journey begun unfolding later. It has not been an easy journey. But it is good to go through the pain and suffering early on. I experienced it all at a young age—thoughts of inferiority, rejections. It was responsible for lots of spiritual growth. There are no worries now. Fortunately, the more I was challenged by my family, by society, the more my spiritual life deepened. I have now reached a certain balance."

"You no longer wear ocher," I observe.

"No. It is clear to me that I'm not going to become a sanyasi. At the age of twenty-three, I stopped wearing my orange garb. I felt like wearing regular clothes, just like a normal person. And so, I did. It took people time to accept that, but now they are comfortable with it.

"One day, a year ago, on one of my trips up north, I actually wore jeans and a T-shirt. I asked one of my disciples to put that picture up on my blog. I wanted people to see what I wore, not hide it from them!"

On the one hand, this sounds like any young woman's sartorial rebellion. On the other hand, interestingly, it is a reverse journey from ocher to blue denim—a spiritual costume thrown aside for a more genuine spirituality!

"Are you ever lonely?"

She laughs. "A few years ago, I wondered if I should allow another person into my life. I mean, a romantic relationship. There are moments when I do feel very alone. But then the moments pass." She pauses and then adds simply, "In any case, I haven't come across anyone who nurses any romantic intentions toward me!"

I smile again at this thirty-three-year-old, her serene self-possession, her effortless candor.

"And when I am in my inner dialogue with Shiva," she continues, "these desires seem irrelevant. What I look forward to more nowadays is a personal circle of friends. I would like friends who won't judge me. Friends with whom I can go and sit and have a coffee at a local Café Coffee Day. Friends with whom I can be myself. At this point, I want human connection more than anything else."

I nod. If it is difficult for most people to come out of the closet as spiritual seekers, I can imagine how much more difficult it must be for a nada yogini in search of friendship.

"After a Guru Pooja, I am often lighthearted, funny, cracking jokes." She smiles. "My disciples enjoy that aspect of me. But because of my practices and long periods of silence, I sometimes feel I have missed out on exploring this aspect of life. I have rejected some important emotions and experiences on my journey—the opportunity to be a child, the chance to be playful, to indulge in certain preferences of food or clothes, so many little things.

"But it is time to be true to myself. I feel the need to abandon typical ashram protocol and allow things to evolve—more playfully, more naturally."

I ask her a question that fuels much of my curiosity about her: what being a woman on this journey has meant to her.

"I see many women on this journey nowadays," she says after a long pause. "There are many on the path of Shiva in particular. It feels like a resurgence. It feels like Shiva wants to bless everyone—irrespective of gender, sect, class, caste, faith. There are no barriers when it comes to Shiva."

"Have these barriers ever mattered to you, personally?"

"Personally, ritual orthodoxy has never mattered to me. Especially rules about cleanness and uncleanness. After the age of fifteen, it didn't matter to me whether I had my period or not, I would still do my poojas. Once when preparing for Guru Pooja, I got my period. I just cleaned myself and went on with it. And in fact, there was none of the pain that regularly accompanies my menstrual cycle.

"A few years ago, I was in Yamunotri when I got my period. I wanted to take a dip and was upset. Not because I thought I was impure, but just because it was inconvenient. I prayed and asked for guidance. And it actually stopped! But there was no religious taboo attached to it. It was just a nuisance, and I was grateful that I didn't get my period that month. Nothing more.

"There is a certain beauty about the actual process of conducting a sacred rite, whether it is a pooja or homa. That, to me, is everything. At that moment, all ideas of gender become irrelevant. I am simply the owner of a body. There is no thought of awkwardness, of privilege, of superiority or inferiority, or of beauty."

"Do you find more women drawn to you as disciples?"

"Previously, I had more male disciples. Now there are more women who help me in my poojas. I find it easier working with women. They pick up things more quickly; they're more attentive to detail."

"How do you see the notion of the guru?"

"I am often asked how to recognize one's guru. I tell people: when you see your guru, your sense of individuality—the 'I'—diminishes. There will be questions, of course, but not doubt. A certain calm will descend.

"Not every guru chooses to be in an ashram. You could find your guru anywhere—on the roadside, even. A guru is just an instrument. Shiva is there ultimately to guide the seeker. The guru merely allows his or her body-mind to become a vehicle through which divinity flows and guides the seeker. But apart from that, every guru has his or her individuality as well—a personality, a svabhava. That is why no two gurus are ever the same."

"Does Devi mean anything to you?"

She smiles. "Though my internal practice is connected to Shiva, a lot of the nurturing mother energy comes through me because of Shakti, the goddess principle. She is a cleansing and guiding force of great compassion. I have a personal connect with Sri Vidya [the tantric science centered on the Goddess]. When I travel within myself with Sri Vidya and my mantras, a lot is revealed to me. It is also easy for people to connect with her. Every time I conduct a Devi Pooja, there are more smiles around me. People find it easier to connect with me when I am in that state."

"And the state of Shiva is different?"

"Very different. Shiva *is*. He never rules. He is silent in his bliss—in Shivananda. If you have lots of courage and karmic support, he will be an auspicious experience for you. But if you are not ready yet, you need Shakti. Only when these two inner forces—the ida and pingala, as yoga calls them—are in balance, will your life will be complete."

There is a pause. And so, here is a woman who confounds every stereotype about spiritual guides, I think. If most seekers find themselves stripping away the superfluities of a worldly identity before turning to the divine, here is a teacher who has had to strip away a religious identity to become herself. From KitKat Swami to nada yogini—it is a journey unlike any other I've heard of!

"Yes, my path has been strange," Balarishi concurs, smiling. "I became a guru, then started questioning why I became one! I missed my childhood. I was not comfortable with crowds, with fame, with the loss of privacy, with the erosion of freedom. Some of my reluctance stemmed from that vasana [predisposition]. When I was young, I often prayed for no more than ten to twenty people at a satsangh. And when I did, my wish was invariably granted! Shiva really does take care of you!

"But now that fear has dropped away. The pattern of

resistance is coming to an end. My world is full of people and conversations. I have learned to be less judgmental of people. Each one is on their journey. If I am to help them, I have to love them—even though I am often aware of the kind of mistakes they are likely to make!

"I see now that the relationship between guide and seeker is mutual. That makes me more welcoming of spiritual seekers. There is such a feeling of bliss and joy after a satsangh. At that time, I feel *this* is my role—this sharing of energy. How could it be otherwise?

"Recognizing Shiva in others is a sure way to feel a surge of personal energy. When that energy is shared, more love is received. When there is no sense of individuality or separateness, even blessing people enhances one's energy; it does not deplete it.

"All the aspects of an ashram are now in place here. Even when I don't do very much, people don't leave me. That for me is a reminder from Shiva that I must not turn my back on this role. I owe it to my disciples to see them through."

Our conversation is beginning to wind down. I know it is a privilege to have heard an entire lifetime encapsulated in four hours.

"When you are with Shiva, even fear is just a face," Balarishi says, as I rise to leave. "You realize it is all right to be afraid. When you are tuned in to yourself in awareness, you receive a beautiful inner assurance that you are taken care of. Always. It can be no other way. The courage to walk the path alone comes from Shiva."

I am left again with the word "Shiva"—that mix of principle and preceptor, primordial essence and compassionate guide.

Clearly, the Shiva of Balarishi's understanding has been generous. The courage to walk alone is something that she exhibits in abundance. And yet, it feels like the warmth of love and friendship that she speaks of is not incompatible with the inwardness of the spiritual journey—an inwardness that she already lives out with dignity and conviction.

And I have a hunch that Shiva wouldn't find Balarishi downing a cappuccino with friends at a local café such an outrageous prospect either!

Tongue

The tongue is alone and tethered in its mouth
      –John Berger

The man in front of me
is reading
a balance sheet.

He is smiling, his gaze
shimmying between columns,
effortlessly
bilingual.

And though a little drunk
on the liquor of profit

I like to think he is not immune
to the sharp beauty

of integers, simmering
with their own inner life,

and I wonder if he feels

the way I do sometimes
            around words,

waiting for them to lead me
past the shudder
            of tap root,
                        past the inkiness
                                    of groundwater
                                                to those places

where all tongues meet—

            calculus, Persian, Kokborok, flamenco,

the tongue sparrows know, and accountants,
and those palm trees at the far end
of holiday photographs,

            your tongue,
            mine,

the kiss that knows
from where the first songs sprang,

            forested and densely plural,

the kiss that knows
no separation.

Tree

It takes a certain cussedness
to be a tree in this city,
a certain inflexible woodenness

to dig in your heels
and hold your own
amid lampposts sleek as mannequins
and buildings that hold sun and glass together
with more will power than cement,

to continue that dated ritual,
reissuing a tireless
maze of phalange and webbing,
perpetuating that third world profusion
of outstretched hand,
each with its blaze of finger
and more finger—

so many ways of tasting neon,
so many ways of latticing a wind,
so many ways of being ancillary to the self
without resenting it.

What It Takes
to Be a Redwood Tree
Lata Mani

When Lata Mani was driving to her office at the University of California, Davis, one morning in 1993, her life turned turtle. Quite literally. A stolen Pepsi Cola truck collided headlong with her on the freeway. As her car flew up into the air and spun several times before landing, much else plunged into a dizzying spin-cycle from which it would take years to emerge: her career, her health, her worldview, her life as she knew it.

It had to be one of the rudest and most catastrophic spiritual initiations in the book. A rebirth that turned things upside down, inside out. The most radical lesson in de-hierarchizing the world. The ground beneath her feet vanished, the mind was stunned into silence, the body shocked out of its illusion of solidity into a state of uncongealed pain and seismic uncertainty. And with that brain injury, everything changed. It has never quite been the same again.

And so, skeptic turned spiritual apprentice. Marxist turned meditator. Scholar turned bhakta.

I knew the old Lata Mani somewhat. She happens to be a second cousin. She also happened to live in Mumbai in her growing years. She was a remote figure, older by some years, inspiring as an articulate feminist of her generation, glamorous in the life of self-determination that she represented. She left for California to study, proceeding to author a major work of feminist scholarship on the debate around sati in colonial India. I lost touch with her after she left my city.

But it is the new Lata Mani that I have gotten to know better. I had my first real conversation with her in 2010. Our connect was immediate, spontaneous, cutting through social natter and nicety with a directness and definitiveness that surprised me. I had known the "outer" Lata somewhat sketchily. I now encountered what one might call the "inner" Lata: contemplative writer, unabashed Devi devotee, a woman of clarity and unselfconscious poise. It was like meeting her for the very first time.

And yet, there were connections with the Lata of old. The lucidity and incisiveness of mind was very much in evidence. The commitment to social justice remained, even if its textures were altered. And she was still blazing her own trail—interior, perhaps, but with no loss of self-reliance or intensity.

"'Falling upward' into the world of spirit is usually a metaphor. But in your case, it was absurdly literal!" I tell her.

"I think some of us are hard nuts to crack, so it had to happen this way!" Lata grins.

My conversations with Lata have been largely telephonic, punctuated by fleeting meetings when I happen to be passing through her city. But I have a vivid recollection of a long evening I spent with her in her Bengaluru flat in 2011—an oasis of luminous quiet amid the mayhem of metropolitan India. We talked a great deal that day, late into the evening, and again the next morning. We talked of family, books, the goddess, love, as well as the spiritual "crash course" that redefined her life. She had moved back to India in 2004—a major transition, but perhaps not as disruptive as the inner shift that had already occurred.

I remember her saying her injury had dropped her into "a new neighborhood"—a quietly laconic phrase with which she summed up this descent into horrifying and unrelenting pain. In her writing, she describes it even more vividly as a state of being "in pre-op for cosmic surgery." The description reminded me of some calamitous rite of shamanic initiation. The experience compelled her to inhabit the body in a way she never had before. Was this a direct insight that happened as a consequence of the trauma, I ask her.

"Yes, it all changed when that desperate young man driving at a hundred miles per hour sought to end his life by plowing into my car. We both survived! But while I survived the collision, my brain was no longer intact. Gradually, I began to experience states of consciousness for which I had no language. I first began to sense the connectedness of everything. I had encountered the notion of a unifying substratum before, but only as an idea. Experiencing it was an altogether different matter."

The injury catapulted Lata into a land for which she had no name. When I think of the ways in which some saint-poets have invoked it (Ravidas's "Begumpura," the utopian land without sorrows, taxes, travails, and hierarchies, for instance, or Kabir's "wondrous city," the land where "fruit shines without a tree"), the descriptions are lyrical. They do not suggest the ordeal, the baptism by fire that can precede it. Lata's term for the land in which she crash-landed is, by contrast, unsentimental. She describes it simply as abiding "isness." She did not discover it as a lofty philosophical idea. There was no flight into the empyrean. No "top of the world looking down on creation" brand of ecstatic high. No out-of-body experience. Instead, Lata Mani discovered isness *in and through her body.*

"As you know many spiritual experiences or insights are first experienced as spontaneous gifts for which we have no prior frame of reference," she says. "Isness was gradually revealed to me in the depths of a brain injury that had made thought and communication difficult. Everything was stripped to its bare essentials. And yet there was a certain vibrancy and richness that I was experiencing alongside the very real trauma of the injury. It was not a state in which I 'transcended' my circumstances, but one in which I was *breathed more deeply into it.*"

And this is the most fascinating part about Lata's journey: the upside-downness of it at every level. Her training thus far had prepared her to look at social structures "ground up," but this was about a "ground up" darshan of existence itself—orchestrated by a cellular intelligence rather than a cerebral one. The intellect was no longer in charge. As the reins were handed over to a more grassroots wisdom of marrow and viscera, the mind emerged, redefined—a democratic collaborator on the life journey, rather than dictator of it.

I imagine this as the state of gobsmacked awe in which Yudhishthira, that great valiant of the Indian epic Mahabharata, might have found himself at the top of Mount Meru: a terrifying confrontation with reversal of every kind. But then other questions begin to surface. It is wonderful to think of some reversals, but not others. The biblical image of lions eating with lambs, for instance, gives me consolation. But what of all our divisions of the world into good guys and bad, the forces of light and darkness, or even our political allegiances to left wing or right? What about our longing for poetic justice? How ready am I for a vision of utter and absolute equality, I ask myself?

In *Interleaves*, a fine account of her tryst with chronic illness (published eight years after her accident), Lata has written of this destabilizing life experience. Every attempt to communicate with the outside world, she says, felt like

trying to send "a postcard from the bottom of the ocean."
No language seemed adequate. Words slipped out of her
grasp as she tried to talk of this interior world in which she
"dreamed, lived, suffered and prayed."

She speaks movingly of irrelevance—of not fitting into
the world of busyness and self-consequence around her.
"There is no legitimate function or place for the chronically ill person," she writes. "Her existence represents a
rupture. She is the spoiler at the party." She speaks of the
kind but puzzled gazes of friends, the "think positive, try
harder" sports-coach wisdom of doctors, the difficulty of
finding real listeners. She speaks too of the temptation
among some friends to "spiritualize" her experience, and
turn her into the friendly neighborhood yogi. Gazing at her
immobility, they enviously remarked that they longed to
enter into a period of retreat themselves. "The craft of sur-
vival was thus at times reduced to the disembodied hero-
ics of a yogi in training," she writes dryly.

At the same time, the similarities between the mystical
and traumatic experience cannot be ignored. Both are often experienced as cataclysmic. Both entail head-on colli-
sions with the abyss. Prisoners of war speak of their
experience as one of "nakedness" and a "war . . . against
emptiness," and Hiroshima survivors speak of "indescrib-
able emptiness," "vacuums," and "a state of blankness."
The mystical experience is described in uncannily similar
terms: shamans speak of initiatory sicknesses, and mystics
across traditions speak of their encounters with ultimate

reality as the illness from which you never recover. A terrible blindness marked St. Paul's conversion on the road to Damascus. "Like a saw / it cuts," says Basavanna. "If you risk your hand / with a cobra in a pitcher / will it let you / pass?" Salabega, the mystic of Odisha, speaks of the divine as a rogue panther that drags hapless seekers to its lair to tear their hearts to shreds. Tukaram warns of the Great Ghost that roams the forest near the holy town of Pandharpur: "O do not ever go there—you! / Nobody who goes in ever comes back." The twentieth-century "anti-guru" U. G. Krishnamurti famously referred to the turning-point experience in his life as "the calamity"—"A sudden explosion inside, blasting, as it were, every cell, every nerve and every gland in my body."

And yet, of course, not every trauma becomes a catalyst for spiritual transformation. Not every breakdown becomes a breakthrough. A blend of agency *and* grace, choice *and* mystery seems to be involved in the transformation of a victim into an empowered survivor.

Lata says that as she breathed deeply into her condition, something unmistakable began to emerge. "I slowly began to grasp this vibrant seam as isness," she says. "And it seemed that the more nonresistant I was to my circumstances, the more fully present I was in my body, the more I felt held by isness. And the more it could teach me.

"It made me unafraid, and for this I remain deeply grateful, because by every reckoning, my situation was an unmitigated disaster. I subsequently realized that most spiritual practices are intended to facilitate our experience of isness. For example, we fall into it in meditation, when we drop beneath the chattering of mind. Isness is the rich fecundity in which our life unfolds—its tumult included."

"Did these insights happen in a flash, or gradually over time?"

"The learnings were gradual. There was no single moment of illumination. And it was all learned in the crucible of postinjury pain and suffering, with my body leading the way."

Lata refuses to romanticize her suffering in any way. She does not tell us it is essential for spiritual growth. "Pain is no more and no less profound than any other sensation," she asserts in her book. "As we breathe into the pain, as we dive through breath into the whirlpool of stuck energy, we experience the truth that pain, for all its seeming density, is no more solid than air." Her realization was not that pain is ennobling. Or that pain is good for the soul. Her realization was starker, simpler: *pain just is*.

The dance between effort and surrender continued for weeks, months, years. There were days, she writes, when she could only pray, "Show me Your face in the grief, my Lord, show me Your face in the pain." And that was when, she says, something else made its presence felt. She now began to sense "the warm presence of mercy, the tender glow of compassion and the silent grace of the Divine." She began to look forward to her daily afternoon encounter with what she calls "the Light . . . falling noiselessly like virgin snow." When it came, she says, "it felt as though I was lifted into a different environment and the body seemed to relax deeply into its vibration. I was jealous of this time with the Light and it never disappointed me."

What exactly *was* this Light?

"I began to experience a kind of love that I had never experienced before," says Lata. "And I began hearing in my inner ear words and poems and songs and invitations that I had never heard before. I had no choice but to open myself to allow this force to teach me. That was when my apprenticeship began. And it has continued."

What I enjoy about Lata's company is the ease with which it segues between the commonplace and the profound. The mix is effortless because in her experience, there *are* no incongruities here. Our conversation that evening in Bengaluru veered from discussing a carrot-and-peas curry she had made and an aunt's indifferent health to an account of her relationship with the Moon. I remember how, when talking of a book I had written, she suddenly paused and said, "Divine Mother is asking me to read you a poem." Being around her, I am always reminded of how deeply the magical imbues what we call the "real" world.

I wonder how this experience of isness connected with the earlier Lata Mani. Was there a connect at all? Or was it a total rupture?

"What I was experiencing in the depths of the brain injury was something for which neither Marxism nor postcolonial theory nor feminism had prepared me. I found myself needing to rethink everything from the ground up. To give one example, for several years my life seemingly consisted of little other than breathing in and out! I had to learn to set aside judgment and shame about the 'value' or 'purpose' of my life.

"Many presumptions dissolved. The secular idea of equality that had anchored my thinking suddenly seemed tame, insufficient to the radical fact that it was not just humans who were equal to one another, but all of Creation. Even the ranking of activity into productive and unproductive was revealed as false."

Lata speaks today in effortless abstractions—a legacy of her academic training. But a chapter in her book makes this point by offering a vivid image that I have never forgotten. She speaks here of a trip to the garden. In her condition, this was nothing short of a project. It was preceded by an hour of meditation, a bowl of porridge eaten in silence, two aspirins, and the decision to postpone a short phone call (because her condition offered her a stern "either-or" alternative: phone call or garden).

Lata recalls plucking some wilted flowers from their stems. This filled her with a deep sense of accomplishment. However, when exhaustion caught up with her, she had no choice but to retreat indoors. More flowers remained. Her gardening was far from over. And yet, that day's expedition into the garden had become, in her experience, a "majestic adventure." She had learned something momentous that day: "the folly of believing that a task is only done when it is completed." The Estonian poet Jaan Kaplinski voices a similar sentiment in a poem I have never forgotten: "The washing never gets done / The furnace never gets heated / Books never get read / Life is never completed."

And so, Lata's "ground up" learning was full of undramatic, daily discoveries. "One of the things about the spiritual journey—as anyone who's been on one would recognize—is that every idea you have about the spiritual journey is turned turtle (to borrow a phrase from you)," she says. "What became clear to me midway through my recovery was that the invitation was not merely to open to this nameless, formless, immeasurable love and how it was remaking my consciousness, but to integrate it with my prior training. What was the nature of the bridge? *Was* there a bridge? What does Marxism or feminism have to do with the spiritual journey? What is it about this new experience that might help illuminate the kinds of issues I was interested in previously? So yes, 1993 remade me. It's still remaking me. And I am still trying to find language."

It is a noisy world. Research shows that in the world of trauma, like the spiritual domain, one hears the voices of men oftener than women. The public traumas of soldiers are ranked as more major than the quieter, more invisible traumas of women (particularly those who have suffered rape or sexual abuse). Between these voices and the hyperclinical conclusions of researchers who link mystical insight to the levels of damage inflicted on the dorsolateral prefrontal cortex, the trauma survivor has to find her own way to articulate her experience. This, as I see it, is Lata's essential challenge: to find a language fresh and supple enough to speak of the decidedly unusual, "inside-out" nature of her world.

She does not deny convergences with other languages. Indeed, she draws liberally on the spiritual vocabulary of Hinduism, Buddhism, and other traditions. She also values the precision of articulation with which her social science training has equipped her. But she is still in search of an idiom that is shareable even while it honors her subjectivity. Hers is every writer's challenge, made more demanding by the fact that it entails translating the particularly opaque worlds of trauma and spiritual awakening into an accessible lingua franca.

And yet, her presence is itself the bridge, I believe, in more ways than she knows.

I wonder at how the Marxist and the mystic go together. Poetry, I tell Lata, is a place of uncertainty, of wonder. It makes for a kind of inspired verbal floundering. It is about uncovering meaning rather than imposing it. So, I understand why the mystic often turns to poetry. "But a Marxist framework, isn't that a matrix you *impose* on life?"

"There are so many questions embedded in that! Let me go at it tangentially," says Lata. "What most spiritual traditions do is address the individual. Obviously, spiritual teachings have valence and resonance for more than the individual. But fundamentally, spiritual teachings address the individual. What I would say secular forms of knowledge offer us is the notion of the social.

"Spiritual teachings are unitive philosophies. When they are practiced at their deepest level what you experience is your intimacy with the whole of the universe. So, it's an individual journey but it's not an *individualist* journey. As you understand yourself as a dancing molecule, you are opened to leaning into, bowing down with, the rest of Creation. So, you have a sense of your connection to something larger.

"But there is an intermediate category which is the social. And that is what sociology, history, politics, philosophy, all of these secular forms of knowledge give you access to. If you are to strive for unconditioned knowledge, you have to understand your own social formation. If you are not to reproduce the cultural conditioning of the tradition into which you are born, or the tradition that calls to you (you may be born into a tradition called Hinduism, and you may be called by Sufism or Buddhism), there is no way to do it without understanding the social."

Those social questions still engage Lata deeply. Much of her work grapples with these issues, albeit differently in her post-1993 incarnation. "How is hate culturally legitimized? How is greed made socially acceptable so that the profit motive and material aspiration are so naturalized that we do not take a critical view of the kind of economic system within which we live? All of this cannot come to you only from the spiritual teachings. You draw on these other knowledges," she says.

"And I am not unique in doing that. After all, a weaver draws on metaphors from weaving. A weaver may also draw on metaphors from farming. One draws on whatever lexicon is available to one. I guess since this was my intellectual lexicon, this is the kind of transcoding I'm finding myself engaged in. That's a partial answer."

Partial perhaps, but it is the kind of exquisite cogency of which Lata is capable. Like many writers, Lata speaks as she would write. Sentences organize themselves into paragraphs as she speaks. Words like "transcoding" and phrases like "multiply constituted within infinite relations" trip off her tongue fluently.

But it is clear that she prefers not to spend too much time talking biography. And she would rather not present her story as one of "individual triumph in the face of adversity." For although her body was her guide on her journey, she maintains that "the struggle of the personal was ultimately a struggle with the social." Her long years of meditation, she says, have been about "dissolving over and over attachment to biography and social convention" and awakening instead to the "loving embrace" of "each moment."

Lata has been present in my life in odd ways in the past decade. Her telephone calls to me have often happened when I have been dispirited for some reason. She has offered me her own distilled blend of hope and wisdom, but without my having to fill her in on the details of my life situation. The fact that I can say so little and yet receive so much astonishes me. She says she works closely with various nonphysical guides, and their counsel often prompts her to get in touch with a person. At the receiving end of these calls, I can only say they feel gentle and noninterfering, but always heartening. She is matter-of-fact about this role. Her guides may be disembodied, but they are clearly as present for her as any living human being.

In the autumn of 2004, Lata and her partner and fellow graduate student, Ruth Frankenberg, moved to India to work on *The Tantra Chronicles*, forty-three spiritual teachings received from five disembodied sources: Devi, Shiva, Jesus, Mary, and Moon. Ruth died unexpectedly of cancer in 2007. But this deeply unusual work, jointly "received and compiled" by Lata and Ruth, was self-published online, and later as an e-book. I am curious about how Lata sees tantra—the alchemical science in which she was schooled by none other than Devi, the Divine Feminine herself.

"Tantra yoga honors the integrity of embodiment, matter, sensation," she says. "To honor them is not to cling to them but to embrace all three as intrinsically meaningful, not merely something to be tolerated, feared, or transcended. Once you accept embodiment, matter, and sensation as a fundament of existence, spiritual practice is about learning what they can teach us. Tantra yoga is about how to live artfully in relation to all three."

"Are most spiritual practitioners in a hurry to transcend the physical? Is that a problem?" I ask.

"Yes, we often approach the fact of embodiment with suspicion. This makes no sense, since the stated objective of spiritual practice is to help us to live more fully, more wisely, in the here and the now. If this is true, then surely our embodiedness should be the ground of our practice, not that from which we flee. If we try to take shelter from the very stuff of existence, we will naturally not know how to make our way! There is a long and dispiriting tendency to distrust incarnation. It is a consequence of having marginalized the tantric core in most spiritual traditions."

"The world does seem readier to reclaim tantra today. Would you agree?"

"Tantra does speak with great clarity to us today," Lata agrees, "particularly given our belated collective realization that we have desecrated nature and our bodies, and violated our relationship with other living creatures, including fellow humans. For tantra, matter, phenomenality, and the body are sacred, and the senses are not something to be feared, but a form of intelligence to be accessed. Disentangling the wisdom of the senses from the distortions of conditioning is a key aspect of tantric practice. That's how tantra restores to our consciousness the truth of interconnectedness.

"The devastations of living in defiance of the facts of these interrelations are increasingly evident. And there is a palpable longing to heal. Tantra as a framework is subtle and expansive, and it can speak to people regardless of whether they are predisposed to religion or to secularism."

"Do you believe tantra empowers us to deal with diversity, with difference?"

"Absolutely. Diversity is a key principle of nature. Tantra acknowledges it and proposes a method of living in a calm and disciplined relationship to it. Fundamentalism rejects this principle. It is suspicious of nature, of humans, and so its modus operandi is proscription and prescription.

"Fundamentalism is on a relentless and self-defeating drive to tame matter, to control bodies, how they are inhabited, what is done with, to, and by them, et cetera. It is premised on an untruth and has no credible basis. This is why one finds it repeatedly resorting to threats and violence."

Lata speaks in a language that is deliberately impersonal. And yet, interestingly, unlike the other women in this book, her path has never entailed a monastic choice. Quite the reverse. What Lata and Ruth shared was quite clearly what she calls "a consort practice." I ask her to say more. Why is renunciation required of some and not of others? Is it a matter of personal preference?

"Renunciation is a central dynamic in all spiritual journeys, but what we are invited to renounce depends on our path and purpose in a given life. There are many mistaken notions about what can knock one off course, and these have led to superstitions and false hierarchies."

The corrupting power of sex is the supreme superstition, I presume. Lata nods, and adds another: a life disengaged from human affairs. "Both ideas distort and simplify a subtle process whereby, as one's path is unfolded, all that would ever distract one from it begins to reveal itself, and, if we are willing to allow ourselves to be remade, starts to fall away. The spiritual journey is a dance between effort and surrender, letting go and allowing to fall away. If we are struggling mightily with sexual renunciation, it may be because this is not what is intended for us in this life. If we are truly aligned with our path, we will not find ourselves in an unabating conflict with self."

"And how exactly does the consort relationship work?"

"Consort partnerships can be either sexual or celibate. The consort dimension is about the intertwining of path and purpose, about two beings collaborating in a shared calling. Everyone's path is a soul choice, not an accident. It has been crafted with precision to enable the learning we have set out for ourselves before taking birth."

"How do you recognize your consort?"

"Ruth and I knew from the moment we met that we were something to each other. Something that no one else had been to either of us. It was years later when Devi arrived that She used the word 'consort' to describe our relationship."

"And who really is a consort?" I persist.

"One with whom one shares a spiritual destiny. Such a connection may have had a past-life dimension, though there is no reason why this should always be so."

"It sounds decidedly more pleasurable than a solo journey," I remark. But Lata is quick to caution against any schmaltzy understanding of the term. "In a spiritual context, a consort partnership is always a triadic relationship. The consort seekers' paths are deeply intertwined, even as each has her own relationship to the divine, the divine to each, and the divine to two-as-one and one-as-two."

"And that can make it even more challenging than going solo?"

"It is more demanding, because it requires both individuals to surrender at a pace and manner that aligns with the fact of their being twinned. The shedding integral to spiritual growth unfolds in relation to each other, and it can be intense and humbling."

There is a pause. "It is also a gift," Lata adds. "It offers companionship in what is otherwise a solitary journey."

I ask her to explain further. The "two-in-one laptop" or "sofa-cum-bed" brand of technology sounds odd, even daunting, to me, when applied to human relationships.

"It is not that individuality cedes to some composite essence of the two," Lata explains, pointing out that each party has to allow for personal transformation to prepare for a specific role on a shared journey. "For example, Ruth was a master channel, very skilled at clairaudition. The teachings gathered in *The Tantra Chronicles* came through her body. But the process also required something from me. My job was to sit in meditation to anchor her, so that the teaching could be received, and to bring her back to zip code once it was over."

While the triadic existence involves a blurring of personal

boundaries, it would seem that the glorious uniqueness of each individual remains unaffected. "Each retains their own particularities," emphasizes Lata. "And over time, both individuals' understanding of self becomes relational in a wider and wider sense." The critical challenge, it would seem, is for both parties to be equally willing to allow for the process of "dissolution, melding, and remaking."

Viewing sex as an impediment to self-discovery, then, can be just as reductionist as equating a chosen celibacy with mere sexual repression. "All this is conditioning pure and simple," Lata agrees. "Sex is like every other human activity: an inherently creative form of touch and reciprocity that we practice with care and attention. Like kneading dough, combing hair mindfully, or gently loosening soil from roots while repotting a plant." Only when we turn sex into "an exceptional activity," she says, does it become a problem.

I ask her to tell me more about her spiritual journey with Ruth.

"Our initial learning took place in the context of the intense challenge of living with the consequences of my brain injury. The schoolroom then was my injured body-mind, Ruth's hands that mysteriously seemed to know how to bring ease, and the teachings she began to receive from Devi as she was working on me. Practical wisdom for and about life was gradually delivered in proportion to our capacity to receive.

"And so, it went on year after year after year, teachings

on the entangled mysteries of life, death, and rebirth, pain, suffering, and joy, the unknown and the unknowable, the quotidian and the extraordinary, the tantra of embodiment. Building from what we already knew and moving at once slowly and swiftly, Devi and our other guides radically transformed our perception. Questions that had been troubling us and others, of which we were only dimly aware, were unearthed and put to rest. It was an alternately exhausting and exhilarating free-fall through space-time, compass-defying and mind-shattering. We finally felt able to breathe into life without ambivalence or resistance."

"Does hierarchy ever enter the picture? We hear of tantric practices in which one person drives the process and the other remains purely instrumental. Is it challenging to maintain an egalitarian consort relationship?"

"Surprising as it may seem, neither of us resisted the work that we were given to do," Lata says. "There is no doubt that our nonresistance was an effect of divine grace. But it was also grounded in the tantric teaching we were receiving. We were learning that in divine creation there is no hierarchy. We were taught that diversity in Creation arises from a collaborative dynamic that involves continual processes of mutual ceding, adjusting, modifying, transforming, harmonizing, and evolving. We learned that hierarchy was a terrible human innovation, that the ranking of forms of life, people, societies, bodies, tasks, et cetera, was the result of human preferences. Surrender involved relinquishing all these misperceptions. The learning curve was steep. But the joy of what we were discovering was overwhelming, and it kept us going."

If relating Lata, the mystic, to Lata, the Marxist, is an interesting proposition, I wonder at how the academic and intellectual sees herself as a devotee above all else. "Where does bhakti come into all this for you?"

"Bhakti is the very cause of Creation. In other words, the world or Creation exists because of the love of the Divine. It is an expression of the love of the Divine. If we think about it that way, bhakti is the first cause.

"And our capacity to love each other and our capacity to love God are simultaneously bequeathed to us in the manifestation of Creation as an act of love. In that sense, bhakti is a kind of pedagogy that is implicit in Creation itself.

"Bhakti is very simply an acknowledgment of the fact of intimacy. Once you acknowledge intimacy, bhakti becomes a disposition. How is it that I experience intimacy? I experience it by opening myself to that which I don't know, that which I love, that which I will allow to remake me and that which I would love to share with the other. If there is something that marks most authoritarian or sectarian or hate-filled discourse, it is the violent act of 'othering.' To other is to deny intimacy.

"It is sad that the word 'bhakt' (devotee) has become associated with the Right in India. This idea that true bhakti is unreflective is deeply problematic. After all, take any saint or any bhakti poet and look at their oeuvre across time. You can see how they are clear about how their own perceptions are changing and shifting. Indeed, part of what they are sharing in their writing and poetic expression is precisely their transforming consciousness."

If Lata's register carries the unmistakable stamp of the scholar, the voices she channels are often distinct in timbre and texture. In an unusual epistolary text called *Radiant Anguish*, she shares her correspondence with a close friend and scholar, J.S., diagnosed with terminal cancer, in the sixteen months preceding her death. At various junctures in this deeply intimate exchange, Lata channels Devi, the Divine Mother, allowing her to speak directly to J.S. The voice that emerges here seems markedly different from Lata's. A new resonance enters the conversation, the idiom turning suddenly more spare, direct, authoritative: "Do you know, beloved one, that one aspect of the journey toward spirit, the Divine, the Self, God . . . whatever you wish to call it . . . the formless One, is learning to see yourself as you are seen by the Divine? Allowing yourself to be held as you are indeed actually held by the Divine? Not in a state of subjection. Not in a state of submission. But in open-eyed, open-hearted wonder. When a child, and indeed all living creatures are my children (I do not infantilize and I know you know this), when a child comes toward me willingly, I am there. I am there. I am there."

I have often asked Lata if she is lonely. She now lives alone, and while her life is abundant in family, friends, and admirers, I wonder if that is enough. She laughs and reminds me of her many nonphysical guides and companions. That is clearly a satsangh like none other! I see her point. I wonder about that company.

"Who is Devi for you?" I ask.

"Devi is my guru," Lata replies simply. "She who came to me in the depths of my illness, and remains my primary teacher, though there are others who also instruct me. Each of us apprehends celestial energies in our own way. I have never 'seen' her, but her vibrational field is unmistakably specific, just like everything in the universe.

"That each thing in the universe has its own unique vibration is extraordinary enough to inspire modesty and wonder. My relationship with her is a source of immense solace, joy, and mystery. Like any other intimate relationship, we have our fair share of quarrels!"

I like the sound of that; it reminds me of my relationship with my guru. I ask her to tell me more.

"In the initial years, it was my dismay at her bargain with free will, given how humans have abused it. But it was really like quarreling about gravity! Free will is a principle at work in the human realm, and one must live in accordance with it. She listened to everything I said and was patient until I got it.

"More recently, it is usually about the impact on those closest to me of the instability of my health, which requires my sisters and friends to really gather around to assist me. I would much rather be able to handle it myself.

But then that is a desire to step out of relationality—and relationality is another principle of Creation.

"You can see why it is hopeless to quarrel! She is always right, though she does not see it as a victory. Nor does she view my wishes for a different unfolding as immaturity. The human journey is complex. Honesty is a prerequisite, as is compassion toward one's humanness. The sadhaka is not one unaffected by life, but one who cultivates the wisdom to navigate it."

"Do you think that, on some level, you might have *needed* your guru to be a female presence, rather than a male one?" I ask.

"I was not looking for the divine, she came looking for me! I have only known her, so it's a bit like my wondering if I would prefer to have had wings rather than feet. I have only known feet. Yet it feels natural that it was the feminine Divine that came barreling toward me. That said, half the beings who guide me today are 'male,' though their 'masculinity' bears little resemblance to what we understand by that term. Language fails one at every turn."

I ask if she has observed significant gender distinctions in the spiritual orientations of those she counsels.

"Gender profoundly shapes our social experience," acknowledges Lata. "This means that men, women, boys, girls, intersexed, and transpersons each carry particular burdens. And all of this intersects with other social axes like class, caste, culture, race, et cetera to shape the nature of our struggles and thus our spiritual journeys. Men enjoy innumerable advantages relative to women. Yet masculinity turns out to be even more oppressive as a mode of existence than femininity. Understanding the social basis of gender helps seekers to fully engage the ground of experience and not merely dismiss it as 'conditioning,' a strategy that leaves undone so much of the work that is essential to spiritual liberation. The trick is in learning how to simultaneously understand, honor, and take distance from that which we have assumed has made us who we are. We are all this and so much more."

I wonder if Lata feels called on to work with other trauma survivors. Although if, as research tells us, 90 percent of all human beings suffer some kind of trauma in their lifetime, I am also aware that her guidance would have to be pretty democratically distributed.

"I don't feel called to work with individuals so much, though I have done that," says Lata, "as much as to write and make work about what trauma, illness, disability, death can teach us about life, living, humanness. As a tantric practitioner, I have been attuned to the body as a temple, a site of intelligence and a source of wisdom. To honor the body, to triangulate its insights with heart and mind and to do so with passion and discernment has been to discover a more joyful and sustainable basis for being alive. I hope my work allows others to experience some of what this orientation makes possible, since they too may find it as nourishing and energizing as I have."

What It Takes to Be a Redwood Tree

Despite her health challenges, Lata leads a busy life. She writes on a range of issues, from spirituality to politics, feminism to tantra. She collaborates on films and multimedia projects. She offers spiritual counsel. She has just moved back to Oakland, California, after fourteen years in Bengaluru. Divine Mother guided her to India. But it was clear to her in 2019 that it was time to leave.

I am curious about what the transition will mean for her. But I am also reminded of an image that Devi once offered Lata to help her through her journey. "She suggested that I emulate the redwood tree," Lata told me. This was when she still lived in California where redwoods thrive. "The roots of the redwood are shallow but the network is horizontally extensive and extraordinarily resilient. At the same time, the vertical trunk shoots determinedly skyward, while the branches plane toward the earth. It is a perfect image for the rooted dis/passion of the tantric way. We are fully present on earth, densely connected to each other, and equally to that from which we came, and to which we will return."

That image has stayed with me. The redwood tree as an axis between temporality and foreverness. Between earth and vertigo. I am reminded too of a couple of lines in Lata's book: "Truth is merciless. It demands that we not set up residence anywhere, but remain ever ready to resume our journey onward."

Lata is obviously no rookie at the business of uncertainty. Preparing for it is the very stuff of her daily practice. One could say she has been preparing for changes in residence for close to three decades now.

And yet, wherever she transplants herself, I know there is one foregone conclusion: Lata Mani will remain her own singular brand of truth-teller, continuing to seek a language fluid enough to speak of wheeling earth and soaring sky, of history and timelessness, of social critique and sacred mystery.

Remembering

Friend, when will I have it / both ways, / be with Him /
yet not with Him ... ?
        —Akka Mahadevi (translated from the Kannada by
            A. K. Ramanujan)

Here's what I'm good at.

When you're around,
marinating.

When you're not,
remembering.

Nostalgia is reflex, a spasm
of cortical muscle.

But this remembering isn't habit
or even sentiment.

This remembering
is a slumbering,

allowing main text to drift

into marginalia,
weekday into holiday,

inhaling you
as rumor,
as legend,

and suddenly, as thing,

superbly
       empirical,

with your very own
       local scent
of infinity.

Let me follow river currents
warm with sun,
the ambling storylines
of green lotus stems
and wooden boats.

Let me be that tangle of moonbeam
and plankton

on a journey too pointless
to be pilgrimage,

floating, jamming,
        just jetsamming.

Remembering isn't an art,
more an instinct,

a knowing that there is

nothing limited
about body,

nothing piecemeal
about detail,

nothing at all
        secondhand

about remembering.

The Monk

(who's been in silence
sixteen years)

writes me a note
at a yak tea stall

skirted by ragged prayer flags
in a gray hiccupping wind

on the road to Kailash.
His face is scarp and fissure

and gleaming teeth.
He spends each day

cleaning his shrine.
"It's worth it," he laughs.

"I clean the shrine,
it cleans me."

He was a spare parts dealer
in a time he barely remembers

before he was tripped up
by something that felt
like a granite mountain in reverse,

the deepest pothole
he's ever known,

too deep
to be called love,

which turned him into a spare part himself,

utterly dispensable,
wildly unemployed.

"And if there is another lifetime
this is what I'd ask for," he says

(and now he doesn't laugh):

"Same silence. Same cleaning."

The Leap into Monkhood
Maa Karpoori

Maa is a sanyasi. She is also a friend.

When I reflect on the fact that my inner circle of friends includes two monks, it gives me pause. It is no coincidence, I've decided. There is something here that I have to acknowledge: I am fascinated, on some level, by monkhood.

Back in college, I had a Jesuit mentor and friend who told me he might easily have joined the Communist Party at the age of nineteen if he hadn't discovered the Society of Jesus first. Nineteen myself, I thought I understood his life choice. As I watched him work furiously on his monographs in his shabby office with wooden ceilings and temperamental kettle, or vanish for days of fieldwork in the Maharashtrian hinterland, I could see the temptation of the renunciate's life.

I relate to the idea (even if I don't feel called to live it) of paring away inessential identities, of giving up the seductive daily jugglery of roles—employee, offspring, spouse, parent—that we are encouraged to believe is the excitement of human life. Outsourcing one's material anxieties to a monastic order to lead a life of social engagement or contemplation also makes sense to me. Simplifying life makes deeper sense still.

At the same time, the Jesuit vow of obedience was a daunting one. I found it more intimidating, I told Rudi, than even the vows of chastity or poverty. With my mistrust of authority, I never quite understood how one could entrust one's freedom to anyone—least of all, to an institutional authority. Yes, I was aware of how "freedom" as a catchword had been mangled to justify, and even valorize, the unconscious life. I knew I was probably guilty of it. And yet, my issues with obedience lingered.

I have learned over time, however, that the lives of householder and monk aren't as polarized as they seem. If you are committed to self-understanding, both lives entail a mix of freedom and discipline. It's a bit like asking a poet which is superior—meter or free verse. Freedom and form are vital to both, so how do you answer that one? In a good poem, free verse isn't self-indulgence, and meter isn't a straitjacket. In a bad poem, they are. The monk as metrician, and the committed seeker as free verse practitioner—those images help me navigate the simpleminded comparisons that often arise on the spiritual path.

Fifteen years ago, in the course of a conversation with a sanyasi from the ashram that I have considered to be my sanctuary for several years, I casually observed, "Monkhood, I imagine, is like a particularly demanding marriage: finding a way to be committed not to one single individual, but to an entire sangha."

Maa happened to be a silent bystander to that conversation. We barely knew each other at the time. But she says that she filed away that comment. It was evidently proof for her that I wasn't just a nosy journalist, an ethnographer foraging for case studies. "I thought to myself then: okay, she sees more than I thought," she says.

Since then, Maa has swept into my life and settled down in it—decisively, as is her manner. She is a significant reference point for me, not to mention an endless source of fellowship and mirth. Talkative and given to theatrical pronouncements, she can be entertaining company. And yet, there is much more to her than that. In the middle of a torrent of anecdote and opinion, she offers liberal doses of insight that, I often suspect, startle her as well. She is a whirlwind: cheerful, opinionated, large-hearted, bristling with dynamism and her own brand of sensitivity.

Maa has been able to propel me into situations I would customarily have run a mile from. She has got me to agree to a three-day ash-gourd-juice diet, to plunge into a chilly temple tank thrice in a single morning, and even to stand on a wobbly ladder to perform a vertiginous snake ritual. I obey because I have learned over the years that it is futile to resist. Maa is a force of nature. To argue with her is like trying to reason with a particularly determined tornado. Or like debating free will with a wildly rampaging earthquake.

She once related a story that gave me an insight into her defining mix of temerity and humor. In the early days of monkhood, she visited the home of her sister, a doctor. The medical checkup took time, and her sister suggested she stay over. The two sisters had dinner and stayed up late, chatting. They turned in at midnight. It was around one in the morning when eight or nine men entered Maa's room. They were copybook burglars, Maa recalls, with knives, blazing eyes, their breaths heavy with paan masala. They surrounded her bed. "I was terrified," says Maa. "But from somewhere inside me, a voice spoke up." She pauses for effect. "I heard myself telling them loudly and sternly, 'Don't you dare touch me!'"

The burglars were taken aback. I imagine them hesitating, mustaches aquiver with uncertainty. Maa pressed her advantage. "Can't you see I'm a monk? Don't you lay a finger on me."

The men conferred briefly with each other. If they had any baser motives in mind, they decided to quell them. Nonetheless, they gagged Maa, bound her arms and legs, and left her on her bed. They then went about their business. "I could hear them moving around the house. I stayed still, watching my breath. There was not much else I could do." Two hours later, Maa managed to free herself. She went in quest of her sister. The burglars had evidently given up when they found that there was little to burgle in her recently occupied home. "My sister and her husband were in their bedroom, shaken. When I told them what I'd said to the burglars, they couldn't believe it. My sister kept saying: How could you be so bold?" Maa chuckles triumphantly at the memory.

I am not surprised. Maa reminds me of the Ogden Nash poem about a girl named Isabel. When Isabel met a hideous giant, she briskly chopped off his head and sailed on with business as usual. When Isabel encountered a bear, Nash tells us, she simply "washed her hands and she straightened her hair up, / Then Isabel quietly ate the bear up."

Maa has all of Isabel's unflappability and courage. At the same time, her innate honesty prevents her from presenting herself as the unqualified heroine of her stories. As she admitted to me later, "When I returned to the ashram, I was not so brave. The trauma of the incident remained, and it was my guru who helped me through it."

Ours is an odd friendship. Maa and I share a guru. But in terms of temperament, background, and interests, there is very little she and I have in common. Unlike my Jesuit friend, Maa's interests are not particularly intellectual. She is more bhakta and karma yogi—a woman of heart and action. Born in 1960, Maa comes from a traditional family in Palladam in the Tirupur district of Tamil Nadu; she is the eighth of nine siblings (four of whom are doctors). I, on the other hand, grew up in a decidedly nuclear family in the big city. She has worked as an administrative head in a computer firm. I am not a likely choice for an administrative position. Not a likely candidate either. It is probably our divergences that make us tick.

Maa's most notable trait is spiritedness. She is incapable of being tepid. And her spiritual practices have not tamed any of her fiery spirit. As a kindergarten student, she once bit a nun. "Bit her?" I asked uncertainly. Maa nodded, matter-of-factly. The nun was administering a smack on her palm with a ruler, and Maa felt the injustice deserved to be checked.

The nun was incensed, and Maa was swept away to the principal's office. She entered Mother Superior's room, scared, but not particularly contrite. Mother Superior won her over, however. "She asked me to come to her if I had any problem, rather than take matters into my own hands," says Maa. "I was so overcome by her kindness that I wanted to cry. I asked her if I should apologize to my teacher. She said: if you want to." That settled it. Maa had been given a choice, not an instruction. She was disarmed. She apologized to the bitten nun, and what's more, touched her feet. The nun was moved, and embraced her, and all ended well.

It is an incident that sums Maa up, in many ways. Volatile and tempestuous, she is capable of dizzying turnarounds. She can rage at situations and people, but the anger dissolves in an instant. She is more bark than bite. (Even the bitten nun, I suspect, recognized the lack of venom in her pupil's canines!)

One of her striking qualities is her absence of mean-spiritedness. Despite her life path of simplicity, Maa exudes largesse. Tact is not her strong point, but generosity is. She has never met me without excavating something from her bag, whether it is fruit, biscuits, or an entire meal in a steaming lunchbox! When I once mentioned that I had forgotten to bring walking shoes, she conjured those up too, and in the right size! Umbrellas, plates, spoons, bags, shawls—these are child's play for someone of Maa's powers. I am never quite certain how these are manifested and have given up trying to find out.

Abundance is Maa's state of being. Monkhood may be about a chosen austerity, but I realize it has nothing to do with scarcity. Before her initiation into monkhood, she owned a hundred saris, she told me. And she is capable even today of exclaiming in joy when she sees someone wear a sari she likes. I once asked her what her hair was like before she shaved it. "Long, silky, straight," she said, without a hint of regret. "And shiny: friends asked me if I used boot polish on it!"

It has always fascinated me: this capacity to express an unselfconscious joy about the past without a trace of wistfulness. It reminds me of what real renunciation can mean: not a narrowing of the heart into cloistered self-righteousness but the expanding of it into an amplitude of spirit. Nothing studied, nothing phony about it.

The convent school in which Maa studied as a child was situated by a chapel and graveyard. She remembers often slipping out of class to attend funerals next door. "I looked at those dead bodies, their waxy faces, checked to see if their stomachs were moving and that they hadn't been embalmed alive by mistake." Church bells even today bring back memories of funeral services.

We talk often of death, Maa and I. We hope, like everyone else, that we can be prepared for the moment when the bells toll for us, even though we know there are no guarantees that we will. In many ways, it is the terror of the death knell that fueled our spiritual paths.

The encounter with the college bully is yet another telling tale in Maa's folklore. Benny Jacob and his mates stood around the college cafeteria, making off-color remarks about the girls. Maa and her girlfriends tried to give him a wide berth.

One day, as she skulked in, Maa abruptly decided that she'd had enough. "I didn't think about it, or plan it. It was just a hunch that a shock tactic would work." She turned on her heel and walked right up to the fearsome Benny. "What's the problem?" she asked him. "Why are you making it so difficult? Are you afraid to be nice?"

Maybe he was just too dazed by Maa's chutzpah. Or maybe he saw the advantage of enjoying female company rather than have girls scuttle away when they saw him. Either way, it worked. The taunts stopped. The girls breathed a sigh of relief. Maa was a heroine among them. Benny Jacob was tamed.

With her pluck, her organizational skills, her love of

drama, her relish of conversation, her enjoyment of people, food, good clothes, and the good life, I can imagine Maa plunging into the householder's life with gusto. When her parents arranged a marriage alliance for her, I suspect that she thought that is exactly what she *would* do. She could have met the demands of work and home and family with ease. Multitasking, I believe, is a word coined with people like Maa in mind.

But then, Maa was too volatile to ever settle for a lukewarm life. Her intensity was always charring. It still is. "If I hadn't found the spiritual life, I would have destroyed myself," she often says. "I was too high-strung."

And of course, I know what she means, self-combustion being the resort of so many women of intensity. I believe I might have burned myself up too if I hadn't found a guided spiritual path, and before that, poetry—fortunately at a time when a Sylvia Plath–type self-sabotage wasn't an alluring option any more. Maa managed to craft her own makeshift solutions, however. So, the dark moments loomed large, but didn't overwhelm her.

During her college years in Chennai, she remembers a barren phase. There were long hours when she wondered what it was all about. She frequented talks on the Upanishads. She took solitary beach walks to a small coastal temple. She spent hours in the evening at the Ramakrishna Mission on her way back to her students' hostel. A compassionate monk at the Ramakrishna Mission observed her

for a few days and finally offered her a spiritual initiation—
something she gratefully received. It helped. But things
still did not settle within her.

Her parents swung into action. A marriage was arranged.
She wasn't averse to the idea. The marriage happened.
Nothing quite settled still. "We were two strong-willed people," she says after a pause when I ask her about it. I don't
press the point. But I have always wondered at this common
diagnosis of marital failure: a union between "two strong-
willed people." The implied remedy is that one person—no
prizes for guessing which—has to turn pushover.

Maa remembers an incident that took place at the time
of her wedding. "It was a small ceremony that we had at
the old temple in Palladam—just twenty people from both
families. It is a grand Shiva temple. The architecture is
ancient. All pure rock, enormous pillars, with many dark
corners and shadowy crevices. There are always several
sanyasis and sadhus around."

As the wedding party emerged after the ceremony, a
ringing voice suddenly spoke from the shadows: "Why has
a mangalsutra been put around the neck of a girl who is
destined for a rudraksha mala?"

No one knew to whom the voice belonged. One thing
was clear: it was inauspicious at a marriage ceremony.
Maa was whisked away to the car, and everyone beat a
hasty exit. "I soon forgot about the incident," says Maa.
"But I now sometimes remember, and wonder about it. I
don't think I was ever meant for the married life."

The Leap into Monkhood

I have tried to imagine Maa's idea of romance as a young girl. I suspect her youthful idealism and the Gandhian leanings she inherited from her father would have made her dream of some version of a Swami-Vivekananda-and-Nelson-Mandela cocktail—a mix of integrity, vision, and crusading zeal. "True?" I asked her once. She smiled and did not deny it. Maa would have done a fine job of helping this life partner serve his mission too. I can see her micromanaging his cause down to the last detail with terrifying efficiency.

Maa *is* terrifying in many ways. What always rescues her from being a tyrant is her sense of humor. She has a feel for the ridiculous—one of her most disarming traits. In the "burglar" and "Benny Jacob" stories, she starts by presenting herself as protagonist. But the ludic mode invariably overtakes the heroic. "Can you imagine what would have happened if these bullies had confronted me? I know how to playact, that's all. I can pretend to be a bully myself, but I'm a mouse!" And as she breaks into loud peals of laughter, one ends up joining her. Maa doesn't cease to be a tornado even in her humor.

It was four years into her marriage with P—a good man in his own way, she says, but who had no idea how to deal with the tempest he had married—that she heard of a yoga class in her city. Ironically, it was her husband who encouraged her to enroll. "He told me he had heard good things about the teacher from his friends. I said no. He insisted. He came into my office to talk about it. He began raising his voice, so I agreed. Mainly to keep the peace."

Reluctantly, Maa turned up after work at the introductory lecture. All she saw was the feet of the yoga instructor. "As he entered, I had a curious feeling. All my life, I'd felt like I belonged nowhere. I'd searched everywhere—in temples, churches, and various spiritual traditions—and had always been put off by the fanaticism and hypocrisy. And here was this yoga teacher entering the class. All I could see of him were his feet. And I had these tears pouring down my face. I remember having this irrational thought: 'How long you've made me wait.'

"And a second later came the thought, 'If Jesus were on earth, this is how it would feel to watch him pass by.'"

The tears flowed unceasingly. "I was wearing a light gray kurta, I remember. It was wet with tears. My body grew numb, my feet went cold. I knew that this was a direct encounter with something I had been seeking all my life—but indirectly." Unable to dam her tears, Maa had no clue what was happening to her.

What was happening was, in fact, the ancient thunderbolt that has struck unwary seekers since the dawn of time. The guru had arrived.

And what exactly *does* that mean? Having nursed a long-term discomfort about the "guru's lotus feet" brand of florid rhetoric myself, I know the misgivings. I know that gurus can seem feudal, outdated, even plain incomprehensible to many. More so in an age of do-it-yourself kits and self-help manuals. And yet, the reason for the gratitude is actually quite simple: the guru's arrival heralds transformation.

Radical transformation. Transformation that spells greater freedom, not bondage; greater responsibility, not dependency. There are effective gurus and ineffective gurus, of course, just as there are real doctors and phony ones. But the gratitude when you find the real thing is akin to welcoming a plumber after dealing with years of clogged bathroom pipes! Your gratitude for such an advent is enormous, and how could it be otherwise? Suddenly, the self becomes a livable residence—a more cohesive, integrated, and harmonious abode than ever before. The Sufi mystic of Punjab, Bulleh Shah, puts it in less scatological terms. "Hold fast to your murshid," he says, because it is he who makes you "a devotee of all creation." When the heart is cleansed by such bewildered gratitude, how can truth stay hidden, the poet asks. "At this one point," he says simply, "all talk ends."

And so, that day in 1991, Maa's life changed. It was a deep realignment. The low-level discontent about something she couldn't name—and which had been an underlying chord running through her life well before her calamitous marriage—now revved up. What's more, it now had a name. She realized she had been unconsciously nursing a time-honored condition, considered to be a malaise by some and a blessing by others: spiritual hunger.

She enrolled for the yoga class. "My husband told me that I needn't come the next day to the program. I told him there was no way he could stop me. The roles were now reversed: he was urging me to stay home, but now nothing could keep me away!"

It was disconcerting. "When I returned home after the introductory talk, even my home seemed strange to me. My husband and my job seemed alien. I was so disconnected. The only switch that was on was my connection with my master." It terrified her. On the last day of the program, she thought she should approach her teacher about it. "I know what's happening with you," he said briefly before she could open her mouth. "Just relax."

Oddly, she trusted him. She knew she could trust him to guide her after that. It was just the details that needed working out.

Those details took somewhat longer than she had imagined. And they weren't particularly easy either. The practices into which she was initiated proved more explosive than she had anticipated. Her connection with her teacher grew into an all-consuming preoccupation. "I sensed intuitively that he'd come into my life to do something for me that no one else could, or would even dare try. I realized he wouldn't hold my hand. I sensed that he could be ruthless. But it was already too late to back out. I had no choice about it. My world was falling apart. I felt scared, suspended in a kind of limbo, and at the same time, I knew it was right. I started hearing my heartbeat, feeling my breath, in a way that I never had before."

She was able to manage her job, she says, but she couldn't bear the thought of being anywhere but around her mentor after work. The discord at home went up several notches.

One day, she was in the middle of a flaming row with her husband. The phone rang, as phones must during family feuds. It was midnight. Exasperated, she answered the call. "Why are you fighting? Shut up and go to sleep," said her teacher's voice. It was an instruction that went straight to the heart. "Wrong number," she told her husband, turned out the lights and went to bed.

At an advanced-level yoga program (with a strong psychological orientation) conducted by her master in 1991, Maa entered a meditative state in which she had the distinct experience of leaving her body. She hovered high above it, watching flies buzz about her face. "It cured me of my fear of death," she says. "At least for a time."

When her teacher conducted a ninety-day retreat in the hills, Maa had no qualms about enrolling. P—and her job— had become distant impediments by now. They had to be managed, but they had become increasingly irrelevant. At the end of the three months, something had shifted, imperceptibly. The teacher had now become a guru. And when he suggested brahmacharya in 1995 for those who wanted to undertake a single-pointed spiritual journey, Maa enrolled.

"But *why*?" I have often asked. "Why couldn't you commit yourself to a spiritual path as a layperson? Why such a drastic step?"

And yet, on some level, I know the answer. The leap is Maa's typical mode of locomotion. She is not the shuffler on the sidelines, the cautious bystander. She is not, as I am, a chronic backbencher, waiting for the action to come to her. Maa dives right into the action. She could see that she had met the man who was her guru. She could see that he was offering her a path seemingly suited to her extreme temperament: a crazy, all-consuming path. And Maa was ready to take the plunge. I suspect she took it the way she bounded up to Benny Jacob in college. On a sudden, but not entirely unreasonable, impulse.

Monkhood was also a way of proclaiming a new allegiance. It was the perfect way to bid farewell to a life that hadn't delivered any of its promises. Maa wasn't just walking out of her home and slamming the door in an Ibsen play. She was slamming the door shut on what she saw as an inherently unsatisfying world forever. It was goodbye to samsara.

"I don't think I'd ever have made a good wife," Maa once said to me. "I'm too fierce. Brahmacharya was a way of walking alone but with support—the kind of support only a sangha can provide." What she opted for, then, was a collective intimacy—not two people facing each other and trying to work out their dreams, but a group of committed seekers, fueled by the same spiritual initiations, sustained by the same energetic field, facing the same direction and walking ahead to meet a common destination.

I know what she means, of course. She is not the first to want freedom from psychological cycles, from rituals of social conformity. Despite the assurance of an ally at every step, not everyone wants to be yoked to a bullock cart; I know there are cows that want to jump over the moon. And that can be most effectively accomplished alone. But what about the warmth and crackle of companionship? The solidity of a shoulder through hard times? Maa sees my point, but says she had to take the plunge. With a living guru, the prospect didn't feel quite so alarming. "I knew it was the right decision," she says. "And through all the phases of doubt, my inner experiences have confirmed that again and again."

Monkhood can seem like a medieval choice for many. Maa is not unaware of this. "I know people see this as a life of suppression. Of denial. Earlier, I saw it that way too. But if I were to be honest, whenever I thought back on some of the Catholic nuns in my school, or when I visited the Buddhist monasteries in Bhutan, or the Sri Sarada Math in Kerala, I felt a subtle calm. I wasn't conscious of it, but there was a vague feeling that this life stood for something important.

"I am glad I tasted the outside life—professional achievement and marriage. But whenever I got what I wanted, I saw it was not what I was looking for. I turned to monkhood when I was exhausted with everything else. I'm glad that exhaustion happened early. I began to see then that the calm I'd glimpsed earlier could be mine too."

I confess there are occasions in the ashram when a sea of ocher robes can make me wonder why inner awakening must be accompanied by so much external uniformity. Conversations with Maa remind me that it is less about erasure than a voluntary simplicity. "We clean our clothes in earth," she tells me. "There is a certain beauty in that." She explains the process to me in detail: soaking red mud in water over a couple of days, sieving it through a thin muslin cloth, ensuring the consistency is right, handwashing her clothes in water, then dipping them in the thick sludge, making sure the blend of water and soil is finely balanced, beating the clothes on stone to evenly spread the dye and to banish the possibility of mud clots.

"It feels like cleansing on a very deep, elemental level," she says. It is evident, as she speaks, that the tactility of the act means a great deal to her. This is not just a skyward spirituality, she suggests, but an earth-nourished one. Not just a journey of transcendence, but of engagement—a messy, mud-stained engagement with matter, the very planet that sustains us. The power of that symbolism is not lost on me.

At the same time, Maa admits that life in the sangha takes negotiation. While community is vital, she says, it can never be ready-made. It has to be reinvented every single day. She remembers asking her guru what the whole business of brahmacharya was about. The honesty of his reply took her breath away. "I don't really know," he said. "But we'll find out as we go along." The fact that it wasn't a prescribed role, but an evolving one, reassured her.

And yet, the challenges were not in short supply. Her guru, once a close friend and guide, was turning into a larger-than-life figure. Access to him was growing more difficult. A small band of fellow disciples was growing into a large bustling ashram. A spiritual path was getting systematized. It was unnerving.

And then came a rude shock. As her mind became a war zone, ravaged by conflict, her guru intervened unexpectedly. Instead of advising her on how she could handle the changes in her life, he instructed her to go into silence. It felt like banishment. It felt like rejection. With a mind creating its own babel of pain, rage, recrimination, and self-pity, it felt like hell. And so, Maa plunged headlong into her encounter with the dark night of the soul.

"I felt shamed, suffocated, abandoned," she says. "I had lost my family, and now it felt like I had lost my journey. Sometimes it felt like I had lost even my guru. There were times I felt like an insect, crawling around the ashram. I was completely emptied of any self-worth. At times, I felt almost suicidal. I would sit on a mound of sand (there was a lot of construction activity going on in the ashram then, I remember) for hours, wondering if there was any truth to this journey, or if I was simply deceiving myself. It felt like death. So much of what we call 'spiritual' seemed like drama. Or even worse, like a mirage. I would get up and move around just to reassure myself that I was still in my body. The only real things around me were the physical activities—the washing, the cooking, the cleaning. And the breathing. That was real. The rest was vapor."

And who hasn't known some version of this scrubland of the spirit? "When a meteorite shatters your home, be

sure god is visiting you," says Tukaram. The inimitable
Akka Mahadevi speaks of the divine "hiding in absence,"
pointing to that strange paradox: the fact that an acute
single-pointed experience of absence can be far more alchemical than presence. This is precisely when the transformation begins to happen, the mystics tell us. It is now
that, mysteriously, attachment begins to widen into inclusiveness, the sticky compulsiveness of intimacy into a
growing spaciousness, the dryness of desolation into a
bracing freedom.

And this was Maa's experience. "I started reading about
the life of Milarepa, the Tibetan yogi," she says. "He went
about like a hurricane, destroying all the people who had
hurt his family. Then one day, he paused and saw the terrible destructive energy he had become. That's when he
started searching for a spiritual master. I'm a hurricane too
in my own way. I know the havoc I can wreak. My outside
life was less eventful than his, but it was still one of internal struggle, of social friction.

"Milarepa's guru, Marpa, was a severe teacher. He
would instruct his disciple to build a tower, and when it
was finally constructed, he'd order that it be smashed and
rebuilt. He did this several times. But I saw that the brutal-
ity of the guru was actually a way to purify the disciple's
karma. I saw that real freedom doesn't happen overnight.
You may think you're prepared to surrender your ego. You
may think you're ready to break your limitations, that
you're ready for liberation. But there is so much invisible

resistance you don't know about. It is like hacking through stone!

"You first experience the joy of finding a guru. When you've been longing for years, this feels like the ultimate gift. In many ways, it is. But it's important to remember that this is the honeymoon phase. Later, the real journey begins when every tower you build seems to be demolished. The guru seems, in your view, to be suddenly ruthless. You doubt him. He seems suddenly unjust, biased, unfeeling."

And yet, the whole point of the path, Maa began to realize, was to take responsibility for her own projections rather than allow the self-perpetuating drama of mental noise and judgment to overpower her. "Initially, in a sangha, you may follow your guru because you're afraid. You're afraid to stand alone; you're afraid to stand out; you're afraid of what others will say; you want to please others; you're just obeying authority. At this stage, there is no real difference between the social and spiritual life. You're replaying the same patterns.

"I saw my guru as my spiritual teacher, but, initially, I related to him the same way I had related to authority figures in my life—my father, my elder brothers, my boss. It was a subtle replay of my outside life. I was playing the same blame games, the stories of nitpicking and resentment. My karmic patterns were unchanged.

"It was in those darkest moments that Milarepa's story touched me. His perseverance moved me. I was tempted at times to leave. It is a common experience. One ego clash, one disagreement, one argument, and you feel enough is enough! You feel you just cannot take it any longer. But Milarepa's story reminded me that this too would pass." Every conflict, she told herself, was just one more tower, one more sandcastle, one more egoic delusion, tumbling to the ground.

"So, I waited. As a woman, I knew something about waiting. I knew about simply hanging on, not letting go. It was a trial by fire. But I could see it was burning up my patterns, my karmas. I saw that this was a sacrificial fire. It was turning my passion into dispassion, without taking away my intensity. Today my fire is very much alive, but it is no longer destructive."

I tell her for the umpteenth time that it is no coincidence that the name given to her by her guru is Karpoori—camphor, the burning of which is traditionally considered to be purificatory. She laughs.

We are sitting on the stone steps outside a temple tank in the ashram. It is a place to which we often return. It affords us a panoramic view of the mountains, the Velliangiris, lathered, as always, in a great white hush of cloud. The lotus pond ahead of us mirrors their stillness. A dragonfly hovers glassily around us. It is one of those moments when Milarepa's eleventh-century Tibet feels a hair's breadth away.

I am reminded of Akka Mahadevi's lines: "Take these husbands who die, / decay, and feed them / to your kitchen fires!" The kitchen fire—too small to contain Akka's aspirations—was clearly inadequate for Maa as well. Not surprisingly, much sacred poetry warns seekers about the subversive business of bhakti. Even a small spark of love is treacherous, it tells us. A simple hearth can turn into a forest fire—terrifying, unstoppable, indiscriminate. And yet, what burns up is only the deadwood. What remains, we are told, is the essential you. The challenge is to stay the course.

"My surrender didn't come easy," says Maa, her voice reflective. "Maybe I wasn't mature enough. Maybe I hadn't tasted enough of what lies beyond the body-mind. But I struggled a lot in my early years as a monk with possessiveness, attachment, judgment, opinion, prejudice, pain. I was so knotted up that I could find fault with others, but couldn't see my own knots. That was a time of terrible disillusionment. I felt alone. Like I didn't belong. There was no way out. No doorway. No exit."

Maa remembers preparing for death. She deleted all the files on her computer, sent word to her guru, and went to bed one night, convinced she would not wake the next morning.

But amazingly, she did. And that became a turning point. "Something began to shift. I grew less afraid. The loneliness began to grow sweet." A line from her guru gave her some consolation: "Think of this as a tunnel; you will come out at the other end; trust me."

"And that is when I experienced my guru's compassion.

He saw that I wasn't a blind follower. But he also saw that I wasn't giving up. And through all my doubts and rebellions, he never let go. He kept pouring his own energy impartially into me, as I know he does with everyone who is willing to receive it. And just when I felt disillusioned, when all my hopes had collapsed, I experienced what he is *actually* about. I experienced the expansiveness. The immensity. My blocks started dissolving, my knots started coming undone. It was like walking alone on a very vast beach. And suddenly, the waves came and touched my feet."

Maa pauses. I tell her the image is a powerful one. She nods, looking somewhat surprised, as she often does, at her own eloquence.

"He started as a friend, later turned guru," she says at length. "And that's when I realized what a tough taskmaster he is. When he put me through a period of silence (which eventually lasted three years), I felt his presence enter me like a cyclone. It felt like I wasn't in control any more. It was like being flooded, choked, wrung inside out. It felt like death. But after months passed, I felt so completely cleansed that I realized that I had actually been washed up on the other shore.

"My brahmacharya has been a battlefield, full of conflict. But when I took sanyas after my three years of silence, I was at ease. The idea of walking alone now made sense."

That period of silence, she believes, compelled her to drop a personal relationship with her guru and adopt an impersonal but far deeper one. His outer transformation began to matter less and less. She began to experience him as the inner presence that guided her explorations into the world of spirit.

The alchemy, however, is internal. Outsiders who know nothing of the guru-disciple dynamic might be inclined to view Maa's life as one of tame compromise. They might see her as a woman subordinated by a charismatic male mentor, her fire doused, her agency stifled, her wings clipped, her free spirit caged. They might believe she has exchanged an oppressive secular world for an authoritarian spiritual one.

But what will stay unseen is the forest fire. The fire that rages through self-deceptions and closet narcissisms. The fire that illuminates the oldest wounds and toxic crevices of human consciousness. The fire that turns longing into receptivity, ache into equipoise, self-annihilation into self-possession. The fire that makes the journey worthwhile.

For bhakti is not obedience, as many believe, but commitment—and commitment not to a person or a belief, but to an unfolding inner journey. And as the journey deepens, one of the most extraordinary discoveries the bhakta makes is that surrender is not one-sided but deliciously mutual. The guidance to which she surrenders, she discovers to her awe, lives in a perennial state of surrender. Which explains all the old maxims about the reciprocity of the master-student relationship. When the disciple is ready, the Divine—previously so elusive, so whimsical—is simply waiting. "The Infinite," as the poet Emily Dickinson says, is assumed to be "a sudden guest," but "how can that . . . come / which never went away?" And this is the essential intelligence of the path of the heart: the bhakta chooses to dance her dangerous, seductive tango with the sacred, only to arrive at the experiential discovery that there *is* no other.

"Silence broke me," Maa says. "It also saved me. If brahmacharya was a battlefield, sanyas in 2003 was like coming home. I have always felt I lacked inner balance. Others seemed to have much more poise. But now if I closed my eyes, I found no one mattered any more. Not even my guru in his physical form. After sanyas, I was no longer associated with him as a person, or as an organizational head.

"I relate to his personality less and less. The world he lives in is beyond me: it feels too big. But then, he has his mission, and he knows how to manage it. I only need to worry about myself. And he has given me the tools to find him, in the truest possible sense, within me. In that inner space, he never fails me. That is what makes him Sadhguru."

Maa is not naive. She knows that submission to authority is politics, not freedom. She knows the difference between being a fan and a disciple. She knows that devotion is about surrendering to love, not power. That true bhakti is strength, not cowardice. Her reverence for her guru is for real. But it is not servility. She once talked of the time her guru stopped in the middle of an exposition to a group of monks some years ago and asked in his characteristic fashion, "Yes or no?" It was a rhetorical question. It was clear that the expected response was a resounding "yes." In the general chorus of assent, Maa stayed silent.

He turned and looked at her quizzically. He repeated the question. "I don't know," said Maa. "I'm listening, but I still don't know."

"A strange answer," he replied, but he did not push the point. Maa appreciated that.

We have often talked of the medieval Tamil poet-devotees of Shiva, Maa and I. I am drawn to their poetry, particularly the license to see the divine as back-slapping friend and confidant. I often quote a poem by the sixth-century poet Appar: "Why rise at dawn and bathe? / Why practice each rite according to the rules? Why perform great sacrifices at great altars of fire? / All this is in vain if you do not say, / 'He is my friend.'" (I am particularly attracted to this one because of my inability to wake early—a lamentable quality in a yoga practitioner, I am aware.)

For Maa, these poems appeal for different reasons. She likes them for the way they speak of vaulting over existential boundaries, not psychological ones. "These poems hold the divine as friend, but monkhood is about crossing even that line," she says. "It is about stopping the game entirely. Your sadhana helps you cross the boundary between yourself and your guru. Once that happens, nothing matters. There is no you or him anymore. Only expansiveness.

When you have a glimpse of that merger—him as you and you as him—everything else is irrelevant."

She admits that the challenges haven't evaporated entirely. "Some days, everything looks fake. I feel I don't fit in. But I remember to hold on. I've learned to trust this journey. My guru's words don't always reach me. But in his silence, I feel the connection. That silence is impartial, impersonal. Oceanic. And always compassionate. It fills me; it balances me."

The dusk shadows are beginning to lengthen. The sky is a darkening violet. The mountains are an opaque silhouette. They resemble a child's drawing—serrated, weirdly forbidding. A cricket chirps nearby. The lotus pond is depthless vacancy. Night arrives with a sudden definitiveness.

"One thing I do know," says Maa slowly. "Blind surrender gets you nowhere. Impulsive revolt also gets you nowhere. Today, I am more relaxed. I simply walk and witness. I enjoy my weekly day of silence, and am allowing that quality to slowly enter the rest of my life." Monday is Maa's weekly day of self-imposed silence, in addition to the month of silence that all the monks in her sangha are required to observe annually.

Around us, the residents are beginning to wend their way toward the dining hall. Soon, the entire ashram will be in silence, punctuated only by the clack of a security guard's stick, or a distant elephant trumpeting through the rainforest. I think of friends in the big city whose evening is just beginning. I feel a stab of restlessness.

I turn to Maa. "How would you describe monkhood?"

"When what is unnecessary falls away, and only what is absolutely needed remains. When everything is yours and nothing is yours."

And where exactly are *you* today, I persist.

Maa thinks for a moment. "Not in bliss or ecstasy. Those words don't mean much to me. But my home is lit. I am at ease."

Maa's image of a lighted home comforts me. What is more comforting is the fact that Maa is still gloriously and identifiably herself. Despite the regimen of the monk's life, hers has not been a path of standardization. She is not a woman in spiritual uniform. She is not trying to conform to some vanilla template of a monk. She still fumes at perceived injustices. She still laughs at herself, loud and hard. Her guru has given her a path that may have deepened her, but it has not ironed out any of her idiosyncrasy. Hers is a path of growing naturalness. "I am still me," she says. "Maybe just a better version of myself."

"Be a lamp unto yourself" was the Buddha's guidance to his monks. Maa is doing just that. And unknown to herself, she offers the radiance of her presence to others as well, as do so many monks and committed practitioners around her.

We have had our adventures, Maa and I. It is with her that

I have witnessed a sleeping temple come to life in the dawn hours at Guruvayur—my first inkling of the auspiciousness and grandeur that is Krishna. It is with her that I have had long conversations about the bards of Shiva—conversations that have thrilled and awed us. When I encountered a moment of alarm at being stuck in the tunnel of the Kailasanatha temple—which is believed to ensure that one's future rebirths are snuffed out—it is Maa's arm that came in to offer me guidance.

"Don't forget to pull me out," I tell her every now and then, usually when packing my bags to leave the ashram.

"Go," she replies. "Write, travel, experience the world, but return soon."

And this, I realize, is what a layperson and monk can do for each other. They can support their very different paths with humor and empathy, never forgetting that both journeys, while differently defined, lead to a common destination. My route may be different, probably more riddled with detours, but it helps me to know Maa is around.

As I travel, there are several times—in an airport lounge, or on my way out of a hotel room—when I think of her. I imagine her making her slow, determined way around her ashram in the early hours of the morning toward the meditation hall she loves so well. And that image is reassuring. It helps me to know that lives can be lived out with this single-pointed commitment. It helps me to know that one can live in the same geographical space, without restlessness, consciously deepening one's engagement with oneself through the dailiness of practice. It helps me to know that there are comrades on this journey—those with whom one can share doubt, discovery, and laughter in equal measure.

It helps me to know that Maa inhabits the planet at the same time as I do.

Let Me Be Adjective

And so, the verb is all.

But I'm not ready for it yet.

I tie knots
every now and then

to dam the flow,
to pretend

I am thing,
I am thing

and to pretend
you are too,

more thing than I,
worthier of being described.

And until the knots come undone
as one day they must,

let me modify,
qualify,

anoint,
counterpoint,
apostrophize,
parenthesize,
invent,
dissent.

Let me take wing.
Let me sing

you.

> I suppose I'm asking,
> like the old bards did,
> to be your garland,

not always tenderly floral,

just a little tart,
a little contrary,

the kind that isn't always allowed
within walled gardens.

But even as I meander,
    let my trail
        be the thread
      that completes the circle
I long to make around you.

Love, let me be adjective.

Afterword

As a listener, standing on the cusp of these varied articulations, I know they are not easily parsed: Annapurani Amma's girl goddess, her dialogues with long-dead saints; Balarishi's mantras that hover on the margins of meaning and nonmeaning; Lata Mani's attempt to send a "postcard from the bottom of the ocean"; Maa Karpoori's impassioned conversations that never quite touch places of silence and melted identity.

Each of these conversations requires us to taste the flavors of vocabularies that could seem alien, unreal. We may not understand them. We may not know what to make of them. We may not *believe* them.

But in a world where languages vanish into oblivion every few days, perhaps it is simply enough to know that these parallel languages exist—fragile idioms offering us their own inner logic, their own provisional ways of refracting the world, their own slanted luminosity.

If this is a book about language, it is also one about attire. A recurrent trope is clothing: Annapurani Amma's nakedness; Balarishi's journey from ocher to denim; Lata Mani's search for a verbal fabric that combines the cellular and the cerebral; Maa Karpoori's embrace of her monk's apparel. There is a process of weeding, of stripping down, paring away needless acquisition, sheaths of unexamined habit, that each traveler speaks of, in order to find herself. There is also a process of crafting a new garment, a new skin—lighter, airier, less stiff, more porous—into which personal discovery as well as insights garnered from other sources and traditions are internalized, woven in. Which makes this a book about *language, too, as chosen attire—a way of wearing the self.*

Poetry is a language of concealment and revelation. It offers meaning as well as a respite from meaning. A shadow-light weave of layering and unveiling.

And that is how I see these women. Not as case histories to be proved or disproved, but as weaves—of sun and shade, semantics and silence, suspended between logic and lyric. Their language ranges from the dense to the sheer—sometimes Persian carpet, sometimes pure pashmina.

On one level, they are part of a quietly growing chorus—one that recognizes the importance of honoring a woman-nourished, woman-vitalized, woman-inclusive spirituality on this planet. On another, they are just fingers pointing, as so many have before, to the moon.

As each conversation unfolded, I found, it was often

quite enough to listen. To pause. To suspend conclusion. To marvel at the variety of fingers, the diverse darting tongues of fire, that direct attention insistently toward light and mystery. Rather than paraphrase or decode them, it is enough, I believe, to look to where they point.

And if one is lucky, drink silver.

Poems Matter

It was snobbery perhaps
(or habit)

     to want
     perforation,

to choose cotton, for instance,
with its coarse asymmetries,
over polyester
or unctuous rayon.

But this, I suppose,
is what we were looking for all along—
     this weave
      that dares to embrace

        air,

this hush of linen, these frayed edges,
these places where thought
runs

       threadbare,
where colors bleed

into something vastly blue
       like sky,

these tatters
at peace almost
with the great outrage
of not being around.

It's taken a long time
to understand
poems matter

because they have holes.

ACKNOWLEDGMENTS

My sincere gratitude to the following:

Jayashree Aravind, partner on numerous escapades; to her and Anugraha Lakshmanan for their painstaking transcription of hours of audio recording; Nagalakshmi and Annamalai, for car rides, companionship, pilgrimage; Jerry Pinto and Priya D'Souza, fellow travelers in varied and vital ways;

Ravi Singh at Speaking Tiger, India, for offering the manuscript its first home;

Priya Doraswamy, friend and agent, for her contagious positivity, her love of the ocean and many things wild and strange;

Gabriella Page-Fort, for being the kind of editor one dreams of; to her and Ryan Amato, for the warmth of their welcome into the HarperCollins fold;

Raghu Sundaram, for harbor.

Sadhguru, for being the discovery that made the other discoveries of this book possible.

SOURCES

Poems

"Home" and "Tree" were published in *Where I Live: New and Selected Poems*, Bloodaxe Books, UK, 2009.

"When God is a Traveller," "Textile," and "Poems Matter" were published in *When God Is a Traveller*, Bloodaxe Books, 2014.

All the other poems in this book are from *Love Without a Story*, Bloodaxe Books, 2020.

Translations

The translations of Akka Mahadevi and Basavanna are from *Speaking of Siva*, Penguin, 1973, translated by A. K. Ramanujan.

The excerpts from Tukaram are from *Says Tuka*, Poetrywala, 2013, translated by Dilip Chitre.

The translation of a poem by Lal Ded is from *I, Lalla*, Penguin India, 2011, translated by Ranjit Hoskote.

The translation of Meerabai is by Rahul Soni, published in *Eating God*, Penguin, 2014, edited by Arundhathi Subramaniam.

Sources

The excerpts from Rumi are from *The Essential Rumi*, Harper-Collins, 1995, translated by Coleman Barks.

The translation of Appar is from *Poems to Siva*, Princeton Univ. Press, 1989, translated by Indira Viswanathan Peterson.

Other Texts

The essay on Lata Mani mentions three books, all of which can be freely downloaded from her website.

Interleaves: https://www.latamani.com/interleaves

Tantra Chronicles: https://www.latamani.com/the-tantra-chronicles

Radiant Anguish: Conversations at the Cusp, by Lata Mani and J. S.: https://www.latamani.com/radiant-anguish

ABOUT THE AUTHOR

Arundhathi Subramaniam is described as "one of the finest poets writing in India today" (*The Hindu*, 2010) and "a unique poet of our times . . . in a league all by herself" (*Indian Literature*, 2021). Winner of the Sahitya Akademi Prize for Poetry 2020 (awarded by India's national academy of letters), her fourteen books include *Love Without a Story* (Bloodaxe Books, 2020) and, most recently, the Penguin anthology of Indian female sacred poetry, *Wild Women* (2024). Her prose work includes the bestselling biography of a contemporary mystic, *Sadhguru: More Than a Life*, and *The Book of Buddha*, among others. Shortlisted for the T. S. Eliot Prize for Poetry in 2015, her poetry awards include the Il Ceppo Prize in Italy, the Mahakavi Kanhaiyalal Sethia Award, the inaugural Khushwant Singh Prize, the Zee Women's Award for Literature, the Raza Award for Poetry, the Mystic Kalinga Award, the Homi Bhabha, Charles Wallace, and Visiting Arts fellowships, among others. She has worked over the years as curator, critic, and poetry editor, and divides her time between New York, Mumbai, and Chennai.